決勝英單

中學必背單字

1500

中學常考
單字集

Junior High School English : Vocabulary

中學三年單字、文法一次雙效搞定！

里昂・著

山田社
Shan Tian She

U0079856

前言
Preface

學中學英文除了背單字,還要記文法,讀那麼多本好複雜!有沒有可以一邊背單字還能學文法的單字書呢?您的心聲我們聽到了!

本書首創超進化單字、文法同步學習法,讓您全面提升聽說讀寫競爭力!

本書除了參照教育部編定的中學生必背單字以外,並徹底分析中學會考、考高中、英檢、托福、多益必考英單,嚴選絕對必背1500單字,再依所有中學文法主題精心編排,單字、文法交叉學習,為中學會考及各種檢定打好地基。特色有:

★ 中學所有「單字·文法」同步交叉學習,提升造句力!
★ 簡單清楚的文法說明,讓您一看就知道怎麼用!
★ 精修小專欄,釐清英文迷思誤區,讓您戰勝考場!
★ 美籍老師真人朗讀MP3,邊聽邊讀超效率!

精彩內容

❶ 全方位學習法,全面進攻「聽說讀寫」能力,培養超強戰力!

所有文法都在中學範圍內,且句句淺近道地、短小生動,便於記憶。詞、句搭配複習做到點線結合。更將中學必背1500單字納入語境例句,突出單字在句子中的用法,讓單字的面貌更加具體,不僅提高考生對單字的記憶力,又能提升文法熟悉度,就是為了全方位提升「聽、說、讀、寫」戰力,讓您輕輕鬆鬆制霸考場!

❷ 中學必學文法 ✕ 中學必背單字1500雙向交叉學習,單字文法全都記得住!

本書採取黃金搭配「單字 ✕ 文法」,雙向交叉學習,效果最佳,先依所有中學文法主題精心編排,幫助您打好中學文法地基,每個主題再搭配中學必背單字1500個,每個單字搭配的例句全都是中學文法的實際應用!讀完中學文法概念,馬上就用例句實際演練,您自然而然就知道單字、文法該怎麼用!

❸ 精選小專欄,幫您釐清英文學習誤區,就像有家教一樣貼身指導!

中學單字、文法雙效學習,再搭配老師精心撰寫的小專欄,是您在學英文的汪洋大海中的一盞明燈,幫助您解開學習時容易遇到的難題及迷思,就像擁有貼身家教專門指導!選擇聰明的學習方法,就能幫助您學得正確又快速,少走冤枉路!

❹ 附贈美籍老師錄音光碟,用聽的輕鬆記住單字!

隨書附贈由美籍老師錄音朗讀MP3,讓您不只可以用看的,還能在零碎時間「用聽的學」,加深單字、文法印象。跟著老師唸,增強聽、說能力,就能擁有一口連外國人都驚訝的標準英文腔。

目録
Contents

3 名詞與代名詞

4 冠詞、形容詞跟副詞

1.動詞種類─be動詞（現在1）

想說「A（主詞）是B」的時候，也就是表示「A＝B」的關係時，A跟B要用特別的動詞來連接起來，這個動詞叫「be動詞」，而「be動詞」以外的動詞叫「一般動詞」。後面可以接名詞，用來介紹自己的姓名、職業及國籍等。

be (am, are, is,
was, were, been)
[bi]

動 是
I am Mary.
我是瑪莉。

driver
[ˈdraɪvɚ]

名 司機
I am a driver.
我是個司機。

businessman
[ˈbɪznɪsˌmæn]

名 商人
I am a businessman.
我是個商人。

student
[ˈstjudṇt]

名 學生
We are students.
我們是學生。

chocolate
[ˈtʃɔklɪt]

名 巧克力
He is a fan of chocolate.
他是個巧克力迷。

2.動詞種類─be動詞（現在2）

在 be動詞的後面，跟主詞可以劃上等號（＝），有對等關係的詞叫「補語」。補語除了名詞（表示人或物的詞），也可以接形容詞（表示狀態或性質的詞）。

tall
[tɔl]

形 高的
I am tall.
我個子高大。

poor
[pʊr]

形 貧窮的；可憐的
I am poor.
我貧窮。

glad
[glæd]

形 高興的
I am glad.
我很高興。

handsome
[ˈhænsəm]

形 英俊的
I am handsome.
我很英俊。

angry
[ˈæŋgrɪ]

形 生氣的
I am angry.
我很生氣。

3. 動詞種類—be動詞（現在3）

1-1

前面說過了，am這個 be動詞要接在 I的後面，至於 are是接在 You的後面， is是接在he（他）、 she（她）、 it（它）和所有單數名詞的後面。

boy
[bɔɪ]

名 男孩
I am a boy.
我是個男生。

short
[ʃɔrt]

形 矮的；短的
You are short.
你個子矮小。

friend
[frɛnd]

名 朋友
He is my friend.
他是我的朋友。

son
[sʌn]

名 兒子
Tom is my son.
湯姆是我的兒子。

notebook
[ˈnotˌbʊk]

名 筆記本
That is my notebook.
那是我的筆記本。

4.動詞種類—be動詞（現在4）

主詞是複數（2人以上、2個以上），代表性的如： you（你們）、
they（他們）、 we（我們）和所有複數名詞時， be動詞要用 are。這
時候 be動詞後面的名詞就要變成複數形了。

brother
[ˈbrʌðɚ]

名 哥哥；弟弟
We are brothers.
我們是兄弟。

teacher
[ˈtitʃɚ]

名 老師
You are teachers.
你們是老師。

they (them, their,
theirs, themselves)
[ðe]

代 他們（他們的，他們自己）
They are my brothers.
他們是我的兄弟。

goat
[ɡot]

名 山羊
These are goats, not cows.
這些是山羊，不是牛。

player
[ˈpleɚ]

名 選手
You and I are good baseball players.
你跟我是優秀的棒球選手。

5.動詞種類—一般動詞（現在1）

表示人或物「做了什麼，在什麼狀態」的詞叫「動詞」。be動詞
（am, are, is）以外的動詞叫「一般動詞」。英語中主詞後面接動
詞。一般動詞也就是動詞的原形，用來表示現在式這個時態。

swim
[swɪm]

動 游泳
I swim.
我游泳。

walk
[wɔk]

名 走路
I walk.
我走路。

run [rʌn]	動 跑步 You run. 你跑步。
draw [drɔ]	動 畫 We draw. 我們畫畫。
fly [flaɪ]	動 飛 Birds fly. 鳥會飛。

6.動詞種類──一般動詞（現在2）

`1-2`

動詞分及物和不及物兩種，它們的分別是在「後面能不能接受詞」。什麼叫及物呢？及物是指動作會影響到他物，所以後面要接承受這個動作的目的物（也就是受詞）。及物動詞後面要接受詞，不及物動詞後面不接受詞。我們先看及物動詞。

order [ˈɔrdɚ]	動 點菜 I ordered a steak. 我點了一客牛排。
horse [hɔrs]	名 馬 He rides horses. 他騎馬。
touch [tʌtʃ]	動 觸摸 Mike touches the cat. 麥克觸碰那隻貓。
office [ˈɔfɪs]	名 辦公室 George has an office. 喬治有一間辦公室。
catch [kætʃ]	動 接住 His dog catches the ball. 他的狗接住球。

7.動詞種類──一般動詞（現在3）

動作不會影響到他物，而不用接受詞的動詞叫不及物動詞。不及物動詞最大重點就是，後面不能直接加上受詞。

wait
[wet]

動 等待
I wait.
我等待。

win
[wɪn]

動 勝利
I win.
我勝利。

sing
[sɪŋ]

動 唱歌
I sing.
我唱歌。

jump
[dʒʌmp]

動 跳
I jump.
我跳躍。

see
[si]

動 看；了解
I see.
我明白了。

8.動詞種類──第三人稱 ‧ 單數s（1）

我、你以外的人或東西叫「第三人稱」，也就是說話者與聽話者以外的所有的人或物。主詞是第三人稱，而且是單數（一個人、一個）的時候，一般動詞後面要接s，這叫「第三人稱‧單數的s」。

fast
[fæst]

形 快的
He runs fast.
他跑得很快。

like
[laɪk]

動 喜歡
She likes flowers.
她喜歡花。

uncle
[ˈʌŋkl̩]

名 叔伯；舅舅；姨丈
My uncle plays golf.
我叔叔打高爾夫球。

hair
[hel]

名 頭髮
Ann washes her hair everyday.
安每天洗頭。

dinner
[ˈdɪnɚ]

名 晚餐
Jim always cooks his dinner.
吉姆總是自己做晚餐。

9.動詞種類─第三人稱‧單數s（2）

1-3

主詞雖然是第三人稱，但為複數（兩人以上、兩個以上）時，動詞不加s。

Christmas
[ˈkrɪsməs]

名 聖誕節
They like Christmas.
他們喜歡聖誕節。

computer
[kəmˈpjutɚ]

名 電腦
We have a new computer.
我們有部新電腦。

parent
[ˈpɛrənt]

名 父親或母親
Her parents know Ann.
她的父母認識安。

coffee
[ˈkɔfɪ]

名 咖啡
They drink coffee in the morning.
他們早上喝咖啡。

popcorn
[ˈpɑpˌkorn]

名 爆米花
Tom and Judy like popcorn.
湯姆和茱蒂喜歡爆米花。

主詞是「第三人稱單數」時，一般動詞規則上要接s，但是也有不在這個規則範圍內的情況。一般動詞要接 -s, -es的情況是：1.主詞是第三人稱；2.主詞是單數；3.時態是在現在。

early [ˈɝlɪ]	形 早的 She goes to bed early. 她睡得很早。
teach [titʃ]	動 教 He teaches English. 他教英文。
hard [hɑrd]	形 勤奮的；困難的 Mr. Lee studies hard. 李先生努力學習。
stay [ste]	動 停留 Tom has to stay at home. 湯姆得留在家。
car [kɑr]	名 車子 My father has a new car. 我父親有台新車。

11.名詞—主詞‧目的語‧補語（1）

表示人或物的詞叫「名詞」，名詞可以成為句子的主詞。通常主詞後面接動詞，所以《主詞＋動詞》就形成了句子的骨幹啦！

exercise [ˈɛksɚˌsaɪz]	名 運動 Tom exercises. 湯姆運動。
cry [kraɪ]	動 哭 She cried. 她哭了。

write [raɪt]	動 寫 He writes. 他寫東西。
laugh [læf]	動 笑 They laugh. 他們笑。
dance [dæns]	動 跳舞 We dance. 我們跳舞。

12.名詞─主詞・目的語・補語（2）

1-4

名詞會有各種修飾詞，其中比較具代表性的有，修飾名詞的 a, the, my, your, that。

new [nju]	形 新的 There is a new house. 那裡有一間新房子。
aunt [ænt]	名 嬸嬸；舅媽；阿姨 Mary is my aunt. 瑪莉是我的阿姨。
cousin [ˈkʌzn̩]	名 堂、表兄弟姊妹 He is your cousin. 他是你的表弟。
piano [pɪˈæno]	名 鋼琴 My brother plays the piano. 我弟弟彈鋼琴。
promise [ˈprɑmɪs]	動 承諾，保證；名 承諾 She kept her promise. 她遵守了她的承諾。

13.名詞—主詞・目的語・補語（3）

名詞也可以做動詞的受詞。受詞就是接在動詞後面，成為主詞動作對象的詞。要記得喔！及物動詞一定要接受詞。

love
[lʌv]
動 喜愛；愛
I love you.
我愛你。

pet
[pɛt]
名 寵物
I like pets.
我喜歡寵物。

a (an)
[æn]
冠 一個
I bought a pair of shoes.
我買了一雙鞋子。

change
[tʃendʒ]
動 改變；名 零錢
My brother changed his plan.
我弟弟改變了他的計畫。

tower
['tauɚ]
名 塔，高樓
They built that tower.
他們建造了那座塔。

14.名詞—主詞・目的語・補語（4）

名詞也可以是動詞的補語。什麼是補語呢？補語就是出現在be動詞，或一般動詞的後面，用來補充說明主詞，跟主詞有對等（＝）關係的詞。

and
[ænd]
連 和；而且
Mary is a singer and she sings well.
瑪莉是一個歌手，而且她唱得很好。

wise
[waɪz]
形 有智慧的
Jack is a wise lawyer.
傑克是個有智慧的律師。

16

hard-working
[ˈhɑrdˈwɝkɪŋ]

形 盡心盡力的
They are very hard-working students.
他們是很努力的學生。

modern
[ˈmɑdɚn]

形 現代的
My major is modern art.
我的主修是現代藝術。

doctor (Dr.)
[ˈdɑktɚ]

名 醫生
My boyfriend becomes a doctor.
我男朋友成為一名醫生。

15.代名詞──人稱代名詞（1）

1-5

代替名詞的叫「代名詞」，而用來代替人的代名詞叫「人稱代名詞」。當你不想再重複前面提過的名字時，可以用人稱代名詞來代替。

brother
[ˈbrʌðɚ]

名 哥哥；弟弟
Nick is my brother. He likes music.
尼克是我的弟弟。他喜歡音樂。

however
[haʊˈɛvɚ]

副 然而
Mary is an American. However, she can't speak English.
瑪莉是美國人。然而，她並不會說英文。

gray
[gre]

形 灰色
I have a dog. It has gray fur.
我有一隻狗。牠的毛是灰色的。

senior high school
[ˈsinjɚˈhaɪˌskul]

名 高中
Jack and I work in a senior high school. We are teachers.
傑克和我在一所高中工作。我們是老師。

feed
[fid]

動 餵，餵養，飼養
Patty and Iris are my friends. They feed my fish.
派蒂和愛瑞斯是我的朋友。他們餵我的魚。

16.代名詞—人稱代名詞（2）

1-6

人稱代名詞也可以單獨當作主詞使用。人稱代名詞分： 第一人稱：自己是說話者之一，例如：I（我），we（我們）。第二人稱：說話的對象，例如：you（你）。第三人稱：he（他），she（她），It（它），they（他們）。

vegetable
['vɛdʒɪtəbl̩]

名 蔬菜
We hate vegetables.
我們討厭蔬菜。

speaker
['spikɚ]

名 演說家，說話者，講某種語言的人
You are a speaker.
你是一位演說家。

USA
['ju'ɛs'e]

名 美國
He comes from the USA.
他從美國來的。

careful
['kɛrfəl]

形 小心的
She is very careful with the patients.
她對待病人很小心。

teenager
['tin,edʒɚ]

名 青少年
They are just teenagers.
他們只是青少年。

17.代名詞—人稱代名詞（3）

1-6

人稱代名詞也可以是動詞的受詞，這時候叫「受格」，也可以稱做受詞。人稱代名詞當受詞時，大都會有變化。

dog
[dɔg]

名 狗
My dog likes me.
我的狗喜歡我。

strawberry
['strɔbɛrɪ]

名 草莓
These are fresh strawberries. I love them.
這些是新鮮的草莓。我很喜歡它們。

song [sɔŋ]	名 歌曲 Lily likes the song. I like it, too. 莉莉喜歡這首歌，我也喜歡它。
cute [kjut]	形 可愛的 The baby is cute. We love her. 這個小嬰兒很可愛。我們很喜歡她。
cake [kek]	名 蛋糕 These cakes are so delicious. I can eat them all. 這些蛋糕太好吃了。我可以吃光它們。

18.代名詞─人稱代名詞（4）

1-6

記一下受格人稱代名詞的人稱及其單複數。例如，單數：I→me；you→you ；he→him；she→her；it→it；複數：we→us；you→you；they→them。

please [pliz]	動 使高興，使喜歡 Mary pleases us. 瑪莉讓我們開心。
know [no]	動 知道；認識 We know her. 我們認識她。
target ['tɑrgɪt]	名 目標，標靶; 動 瞄準 Target it. 瞄準它。
hate [het]	動 討厭 Lucy hates him. 露西恨他。
tell [tɛl]	動 告訴 Don't tell them. 別告訴他們。

19.形容詞─兩種用法（1）

表示人或物的性質、形狀及數量的詞叫形容詞。形容詞接在名詞的前面，可以修飾後面的名詞，讓後面的名詞有更清楚的表現。

singer
['sɪŋɚ]

名 歌手
She is a good singer.
她是一個很好的歌手。

river
['rɪvɚ]

名 河流
This city has a long river.
這城市有一條很長的河川。

four
[for]

名 四
I have four brothers.
我有四個兄弟。

big
[bɪg]

形 大的
That is a big car.
那是一輛大車子。

interesting
['ɪntrɪstɪŋ]

形 有趣的
This is an interesting book.
這是一本有趣的書。

20.形容詞─兩種用法（2）

一個名詞前面可以有多個形容詞來修飾。

blue
[blu]

名 藍色
I have a beautiful blue ring.
我有一個美麗的藍色戒指。

girl
[gɝl]

名 女孩
She is a big, tall girl.
她是個又高又大的女孩。

young
[jʌŋ]

形 年輕的
The two young boys are my brothers.
這兩個年輕男孩是我的弟弟。

kind
[kaɪnd]

名 種類；形 仁慈的
Jack is a kind and cute boy.
傑克是一個善良又可愛的男孩。

beautiful
[ˈbjutəfəl]

形 美麗的
Ruby is a beautiful young lady.
露比是一個漂亮的年輕少女

21.形容詞—兩種用法（3）

1-7

形容詞也可以當作 be動詞的補語。這時候，只要把形容詞接在be動詞的後面就行了，後面不用接名詞。就像這樣：《主詞＋be動詞＋形容詞》，這裡的形容詞是用來修飾前面的主詞。

fantastic
[fænˈtæstɪk]

形 很棒的
Jane is fantastic.
珍很棒。

doll
[dɑl]

名 洋娃娃
The doll is lovely.
這玩偶很可愛。

sister
[ˈsɪstɚ]

名 姊姊；妹妹
My sister looks happy.
我妹妹看起來很快樂。

old
[old]

形 舊的
That building is old.
那棟建築物很老舊。

famous
[ˈfeməs]

形 有名的
He is very famous.
他非常有名。

22.副詞—讓表現更豐富（1）

用來修飾動詞，表示動作「在哪裡」、「怎麼樣」、「什麼程度」、「在什麼時候」等各種意思的詞叫「副詞」。

throw
[θro]

動 丟，投擲
I throw hard.
我丟得很用力。

speak
[spik]

動 講話
He speaks English slowly.
他慢慢地說英文。

work
[wɜk]

名 工作
She works hard.
她工作努力。

up
[ʌp]

副 起來
I got up early.
我起得早。

eat
[it]

動 吃
Kate eats a lot!
凱特吃很多!

23.副詞—讓表現更豐富（2）

副詞不僅修飾動詞，也可以放在形容詞前面修飾形容詞。

bridge
[brɪdʒ]

名 橋樑
That is a very long bridge.
那是一座很長的橋。

easy
['izɪ]

形 容易的
The test was very easy.
這考試很簡單。

enough
[ɪˈnʌf]

形 足夠的
This beer is cool enough.
這啤酒已經夠涼了。

lazy
[ˈlezɪ]

形 懶惰的
You are too lazy.
你太懶散了。

than
[ðæn]

連 比
Mary is much taller than my sister.
瑪莉比我妹妹高多了。

24.否定文─be動詞（1）

1-8

be動詞（am, are, is）的否定句，就是在be動詞的後面放not，表示「不…」的否定意義。

engineer
[ˌɛndʒəˈnɪr]

名 工程師，技師
I am not George the engineer.
我不是工程師喬治。

Englishman
[ˈɪŋglɪʃmən]

名 英國人
He is not an Englishman.
他不是個英國人。

niece
[nis]

名 姪女，外甥女
You are not his niece.
妳不是他的姪女。

shirt
[ʃɝt]

名 襯衫
This is not my shirt.
這不是我的襯衫。

pig
[pɪg]

名 豬
It is not a pig.
牠不是一隻豬。

25. 否定文─be動詞（2）

be動詞的否定文常用縮寫的形式，要記住喔！isn't是is not的縮寫；aren't是are not的縮寫。

stupid
['stjupɪd]
形 愚蠢；笨
I'm not stupid.
我不笨。

heavy
['hɛvɪ]
形 重的
He's not heavy.
他不重。

smart
[smɑrt]
形 聰明的
Louis isn't smart.
路易斯不聰明。

fat
[fæt]
形 肥胖
You are not fat.
你不胖。

baseball
['besbɔl]
名 棒球
We aren't baseball players.
我們不是棒球選手。

26. 否定文─一般動詞（3）

表示「不…」的否定說法叫「否定句」。一般動詞的否定句的作法，是要在動詞前面加do not（=don't）。do not是現在否定式。

read
[rid]
動 閱讀
I don't read books.
我不看書。

city
['sɪtɪ]
名 城市
You don't like this city.
你不喜歡這個城市。

study ['stʌdɪ]	動 學習 They don't study English. 他們不念英語。
breakfast ['brɛkfəst]	名 早餐 We don't eat breakfast. 我們不吃早餐。
pen [pɛn]	名 鋼筆；原子筆 You don't have a pen. 你沒有筆。

27.否定文──一般動詞（4）

1-9

主詞是「第三人稱‧單數」時，do要改成does，而does not（=doesn't）後面接的動詞一定要是原形動詞。does not是現在否定式。

tennis ['tɛnɪs]	名 網球 She doesn't play tennis. 她不打網球。
music ['mjuzɪk]	名 音樂 He doesn't like music. 他不喜歡音樂。
any ['ɛnɪ]	形 任何的 She doesn't have any brothers. 她沒有任何兄弟。
novel ['nɑvl̩]	形 小說 She doesn't read novels. 她不看小說。
have [hæv]	動 有 Kitty doesn't have a book. 凱蒂沒有書。

28. 疑問句—be動詞（1）

be動詞的疑問句，只把主詞跟動詞前後對調就好啦！也就是《be動詞＋主詞…》，然後句尾標上「？」。配合主詞，要正確加上be動詞喔！回答的方式是：「Yes, 代名詞+ am/are/is.」、「No, 代名詞+am not/aren't/isn't」。

nurse
[nɝs]

名 護士
Are you a nurse?—Yes, I am.
你是護士嗎？－是，我是。

American
[ə'mɛrɪkən]

形 美國（人）的；名 美國人
Are you American?—No, I'm not.
你是美國人嗎？－不，我不是。

uniform
['junə‚fɔrm]

名 制服
Is this your uniform?—Yes, it is.
這是你的制服嗎？－是，它是。

round
[raʊnd]

形 圓的
Is the Earth round?—Yes, it is.
地球是圓的嗎？－是，它是。

park
[pɑrk]

名 公園；動 停車
Is that a park?—Yes, it is.
那是座公園嗎？－是，它是。

29. 疑問句—be動詞（2）

會問問題也要會回答喔！回答疑問句，要把主詞改成人稱代名詞。

celebrate
['sɛlə‚bret]

動 慶祝
Does Ann celebrate Christmas?—No, she doesn't.
安慶祝聖誕節嗎？－不，她不慶祝。

unhappy
[ʌn'hæpɪ]

形 不開心
Is Mary unhappy?—No, she isn't.
瑪莉不開心嗎？－不，她沒有。

healthy ['hɛlθɪ]	形 健康的 Is your sister healthy?—Yes, she is. 你姊姊健康嗎？—是，她健康。
those [ðoz]	代 那些；形 那些 Are those children yours?—No, they aren't. 那些都是你的小孩嗎？—不，他們不是。
smoke [smok]	動 抽煙 Are those boys smoking?—Yes, they are. 那些男孩正在抽煙嗎？—是，他們在抽煙。

30.疑問句——一般動詞（3）

1-10

表示「…嗎？」問對方事物的句子叫「疑問句」。一般動詞的疑問句是在句首接Do，句尾標上「？」。回答的方式是：「Yes, 代名詞+ do.」、「No, 代名詞+ don't」。

comic ['kɑmɪk]	名 漫畫 Do you like comic books?—Yes, I do. 你喜歡漫畫書嗎？—是，我喜歡。
live [lɪv]	動 住 Do you live in New York? —No, I don't. 你住在紐約嗎？—不，我不住那裡。
use [juz]	動 使用 Do you use a computer? —Yes, I do. 你用電腦嗎？—是，我用。
save [sev]	動 節省 Do they save money? —Yes, they do. 他們存錢嗎？—是，他們存錢。
drink [drɪŋk]	動 喝 Do they drink water? —No, they don't. 他們喝水嗎？—不，他們不喝。

31.疑問句——一般動詞（4）

主詞是「第三人稱單數」時，不用do而是用does，而且後面的動詞不加-s, -es，一定要用原形喔！回答的方式是：「Yes, 代名詞+ does.」、「No, 代名詞+ doesn't」。

steak
[stek]

名 牛排

Does Mary like steak?—Yes, she does.
瑪莉喜歡牛排嗎？—是的，她喜歡。

brown
[braʊn]

形 棕色的

Does he have brown eyes?—No, he doesn't.
他有褐色的眼睛嗎？—不，他沒有。

understand
[ʌndɚˈstænd]

動 了解

Does your brother understand English?—Yes, he does.
你弟弟懂英語嗎？—是，他懂。

Taiwan
[ˈtaɪˈwɑn]

名 台灣

Does Ann live in Taiwan?—No, she doesn't.
安住在台灣嗎？—不，她不在。

taste
[test]

動 品嘗

Does it taste good?—Yes, it does.
那吃起來好吃嗎？—是，好吃。

1.過去式——be動詞（1）

要表達動作或情況是發生在過去的時候，英語的動詞是要改成「過去式」的！be動詞的過去式有兩個，am, is的過去形是was，are的過去形是were。

busy
[ˈbɪzɪ]

形 忙碌的

I was busy yesterday.
昨天我很忙。

tired
[taɪrd]

形 累的

She was tired last night.
她昨天晚上很累。

yesterday
['jɛstɚ,de]

名 昨天
You were absent yesterday.
你昨天沒來。

there
[ðɛr]

副 那裡
There were some girls there.
當時那裡有幾個女孩。

week
[wik]

名 星期
We were in Seoul last week.
上星期我們在首爾。

2.過去式—be動詞（2）

`1-11`

表示過去並沒有發生某動作或某狀況時，就要用「過去否定式」。be動詞的「過去」否定式，就是在was或were的後面加上not，成為was not（=wasn't），were not（=weren't）。

reporter
[rɪ'portə]

名 記者，報告人
The reporter was not tired.
那記者當時不累。

married
['mærɪd]

形 已結婚
He wasn't married.
他當時未婚。

bookstore
['bʊk,stor]

名 書店
She wasn't at the bookstore.
她當時不在書店。

afraid
[ə'fred]

形 害怕
They weren't afraid.
他們當時不害怕。

town
[taʊn]

名 市鎮
We weren't in town last week.
上星期我們不在鎮上。

3.過去式─be動詞（3）

be動詞的疑問句，是把be動詞放在主詞的前面，變成《be動詞＋主語…？》，過去式也是一樣喔！回答是用 "yes" 、 "no" 開頭。

flat [flæt]	形 平坦的 Was the road flat?—No, it wasn't. 馬路平坦嗎？—不，不平。
hungry ['hʌŋgrɪ]	形 飢餓的 Were you hungry?—No, I wasn't. 你那時餓嗎？—不，我不餓。
home [hom]	名 家 Were you at home last night—Yes, I was. 你昨晚在家嗎？—是，我在。
rainy ['renɪ]	形 多雨的 Was it rainy in Taipei yesterday?—Yes, It was. 昨天台北一直下雨嗎？—是，一直下雨。
rose [roz]	名 玫瑰 Were the roses pretty?—Yes, they were. 那些玫瑰花漂亮嗎？—是，它們漂亮。

4.過去式──一般動詞（1）

英語中說過去的事時，要把動詞改為過去式。一般動詞的過去形，是在原形動詞的詞尾加上-ed。

help [hɛlp]	動 幫助 She helped me. 她幫了我。
check [tʃɛk]	動 查閱；名 帳單 I checked his homework. 我檢查了他的作業。

night
[naɪt]

名 夜晚的
We danced last night.
我們昨晚跳舞。

watch
[watʃ]

名 手錶；動 看
They watched TV last Sunday.
他們上星期天看了電視。

Monday
['mʌnde]

名 星期一
My mother used my bag last Monday.
我母親上個星期一用了我的包包。

5.過去式——一般動詞（2）

1-12

原則上一般動詞是在詞尾加-ed的，但也有在這原則之外的。如字尾是e直接加d；字尾是子音＋y則去y加 "-ied"；字尾是短母音＋子音的單音節動詞：重複字尾再加 "-ed"，

center
['sɛntɚ]

名 中心
I lived in the center of the city.
我住在市中心。

road
[rod]

名 道路
They decided to clean the road.
他們決定了要清理馬路。

correct
[kə'rɛkt]

動 改正
He grabbed a pen and then corrected the tests.
他抓了一枝筆然後改了考卷。

copy
['kɑpɪ]

名 副本；動 複製
They copied my homework!
他們抄我的作業！

marry
['mærɪ]

動 參與
John married her a month ago.
約翰一個月前娶了她。

6.過去式──一般動詞（3）

一般動詞的過去式中，詞尾不是規則性地接-ed，而是有不規則變化的動詞。這樣的動詞不僅多，而且大都很重要，要一個個確實記住喔！

couch
[kaʊtʃ]

名 躺椅
I bought a couch yesterday.
我昨天買了個躺椅。

sad
[sæd]

形 傷心的
I wrote a sad story.
我寫了一個悲傷的故事。

daughter
[ˈdɔtɚ]

名 女兒
My daughter drew a picture.
我女兒畫了一張畫。

present
[ˈprɛznt]

名 禮物
Mary gave George a present.
瑪莉送了一份禮物給喬治。

table
[ˈtebl]

名 桌子
Kay sat on the table.
凱坐在桌子上。

7.過去式──一般動詞（4）

上述的動詞叫「不規則動詞」，與其相對的，詞尾可直接接-ed變成過去式的就叫做「規則動詞」。

cook
[kʊk]

動 烹飪；名 廚師
She cooked dinner.
她做了晚餐。

dish
[dɪʃ]

名 盤子
I washed the dishes.
我洗了盤子。

house
[haʊs]

名 房子
My children wanted a bigger house.
我的孩子們想要大一點的房子。

some
[sʌm]

形 一些
I used some eggs.
我用了一些蛋。

join
[dʒɔɪn]

動 參與
We joined a new club yesterday.
我們昨天新加入了一個社團。

8. 過去式──一般動詞（5）

要說「我過去沒有做什麼、沒有怎麼樣」，就要用過去否定的說法。一般動詞的「過去」否定，是要在動詞的前面接did not（=didn't）。訣竅是無論主語是什麼，都只要接did就可以啦！

last
[læst]

形 最後的
I didn't watch TV last night.
我昨晚沒有看電視。

book
[buk]

名 書本
I didn't read the book.
我沒看這本書。

come
[kʌm]

動 來
She didn't come.
她沒有來。

bus
[bʌs]

名 公共汽車
He didn't catch the last bus.
他沒有趕上末班公車。

hotel
[ho'tɛl]

名 飯店
We didn't stay at the hotel.
我們並沒有待在飯店裡。

9.過去式——一般動詞（6）

一般動詞的「過去」疑問句，要把Did放在句首，變成《Did＋主詞＋原形動詞…？》。

gift
[gɪft]

名 禮物
Did you receive the gift yesterday?—No, I didn't.
你昨天收到禮物了嗎？—不，我沒有。

husband
[ˈhʌzbənd]

名 丈夫
Did your husband wash the dishes?—No, he didn't.
你的老公有沒有洗碗盤？—不，他沒有。

kiss
[kɪs]

動 吻
Did he kiss her last night?—Yes, he did.
他昨晚有沒有親吻她？—是的，他有。

finish
[ˈfɪnɪʃ]

動 完成
Did you finish your homework?—No, I didn't.
你已經寫完你的作業了嗎？—不，我沒有。

purple
[ˈpɝpl̩]

名 紫色
Did she pick the purple one?—Yes, she did.
她是否選了紫色的那個？—是，她選了。

10.進行式—正在…（1）

《be動詞＋…ing》表示動作正在進行中。…ing是動詞詞尾加ing的形式。現在進行式，用be動詞的現在式，表示「（現在）正在…」的意思；過去進行式，用be動詞的過去式，表示「（那時候）在做…」的意思。

library
[ˈlaɪ,brɛrɪ]

名 圖書館
I am walking to the library.
我正在走路到圖書館。

list
[lɪst]

名 目錄
Helen is making a name list.
海倫正在列名單。

beef
[bif]

名 牛肉
We are cooking beef now.
我們現在正在煮牛肉。

start
[stɑrt]

動 開始
We were just starting the game.
我們當時才正要開始比賽。

boss
[bɔs]

名 老闆
She was talking to her boss.
她當時正在和老闆說話。

小專欄

動詞後面接ing時叫「ing形」，ing形的接法跟規則動詞「ed」的接法很相似。ing形的接法如下：

1.詞尾直接接ing
2.詞尾是e的動詞，去e加ing
3.詞尾是「短母音＋子音」的動詞，子音要重複一次，再加ing。

1.詞尾直接接ing

He is playing soccer now.
他現在正在踢足球。

2.詞尾是e的動詞，去e加ing

I am making a cake.
我正在做蛋糕。

3.詞尾是「短母音＋子音」的動詞，子音要重複一次，再加ing。

We were running with his dog.
我們那時正跟著他的狗跑。

11.進行式—正在…（2）

要說現在並沒有正在做什麼動作，就用進行式的否定形。進行式的否定句是在be動詞的後面接not。這跟be動詞否定句是一樣的。順序是《be動詞＋not＋…ing》，這跟be動詞的否定句是一樣的。

lie
[laɪ]

名 謊話；動 說謊
I'm not lying!
我並沒有在說謊!

lunch
[lʌntʃ]

名 午餐
She isn't cooking lunch.
她沒有在做午餐。

buy
[baɪ]

動 買
They aren't buying a new house.
他們沒有要買新房子。

talk
[tɔk]

動 講話；談話
We weren't talking with Ann.
我們那時沒有在跟安說話。

bath
[bæθ]

動 洗澡
He wasn't taking a bath.
他那時沒有在洗澡。

12.進行式—正在…（3）

進行式的疑問句，是把be動詞放在主詞的前面，順序是《be動詞＋主詞＋…ing？》，這跟be動詞的疑問句也是一樣的。

listen
[ˈlɪsn̩]

動 聆聽
Are you listening?—Yes, I am.
你在聽嗎?—是的，我在聽。

move
[muv]

動 移動；搬
Is she moving the table?—No, she isn't.
她在移動桌子嗎？—不，她沒有。

now	副 現在
[naʊ]	Is it raining now?—Yes, it is.
	現在正在下雨嗎？—是的，正在下。

with	介 和～在一起
[wið]	Were they coming with Tom?—Yes, they were.
	他們那時跟湯姆一起來嗎？—是的，他們有。

time	名 時間
[taɪm]	Were you cooking at that time?—No, I wasn't.
	你那時候在做飯嗎？—沒有，我沒有。

13.未來式（1）

1-15

在英語中要提到「未來」的事，例如未來的夢想、預定或計畫…等，動詞不用變化，而是用《will＋動詞原形》，表示「會…」、「將要…」。這叫「單純未來」。

tomorrow	副 明天
[tə'maro]	He will come tomorrow.
	他明天會到。

will (would)	助 要；將要
[wɪl]	He will be busy tomorrow.
	他明天會很忙。

month	名 月份
[mʌnθ]	We will have exams next month.
	下個月我們有考試。

back	形 後面；回來
[bæk]	They will be right back.
	他們馬上就回來。

it (its，itself)	代 它（它的，它自己）
[ɪt]	It will rain tomorrow.
	明天會下雨。

14.未來式（2）

這個will是表示將來的助動詞，它還有表示未來將發生的動作或狀態，相當於「（未來）將做⋯」的意思。這叫「意志未來」。

tonight
[tə'naɪt]

副 今晚
I will go to the soccer game tonight.
我準備去看今晚的足球賽。

meeting
['mitɪŋ]

名 會議
I will attend the meeting.
我會參加會議。

end
[ɛnd]

動 結束
I will end this conversation.
我準備結束這個對話。

mail
[mel]

名 郵件
She will get the mail.
她會收到郵件。

after
['æftɚ]

介 在～之後
We will call on him after school.
我們下課後準備去他家。

15.未來式（3）

未來式的否定句是把not放在助動詞will的後面，變成《will not +動詞原形》的形式。助動詞跟原形動詞之間插入not成為否定句，可以應用在所有的助動詞上喔！對了，will not的縮寫是won't。

go
[go]

動 去
I won't go to the party.
我不準備去參加宴會。

pack
[pæk]

名 包裹
You will not find a pack of cigarettes here.
你在這裡不會找到一包煙。

window
['wɪndo]

名 窗戶

She won't clean the windows.
她不願打掃窗戶。

child
[tʃaɪld]

名 小孩

My children won't bathe.
我家小孩不洗澡。

Sunday
['sʌnde]

名 星期日

They won't work on Sunday.
他們星期天不工作。

16. 未來式（4）

1-16

be動詞的未來形，跟一般動詞的作法是一樣的。be動詞的（am, are, is）的原形是「be」，所以一般句子是《will be…》，否定句是《will not be…》。

next
[nɛkst]

形 其次的；緊接的

I'll be twenty next month.
我下星期就二十歲了。

hope
[hop]

動 希望

I hope you will be happy here.
希望你在此一切滿意。

late
[let]

形 遲的；晚的

You will be late.
你會遲到。

not
[nɑt]

副 不是；不會

He will not be here on time.
他不會準時到這裡。

here
[hɪr]

副 這裡

I won't be here tomorrow.
我明天不會在這裡。

每個人都喜歡詢問未來。英語中的未來式的疑問句，是將will放在主詞的前面，變成《will+主詞+動詞原形…？》的形式，相當於「會…嗎？」的意思。回答的方式是《Yes, 代名詞+will.》、《No, 代名詞+won't.》

yes (yeah)
[jɛs]

副 是；是的

Will he go abroad?—Yes, he will.
他會出國嗎？—是的，他會。

send
[sɛnd]

動 寄送

Will Jim have time to send the letter? —Yes, he will.
吉姆有時間寄那封信嗎？—有，他有。

arrive
[ə'raɪv]

動 到達

Will we arrive in Tokyo on time? —No, we won't.
我們會準時到東京嗎？—不，我們不會。

call
[kɔl]

動 打（電話）

Will you call me? —Yes, I will.
你會打給我嗎？—會的，我會。

microwave
['maɪkro,wev]

名 微波爐，微波

Will you buy a microwave? —Yes, I will.
你會買個微波爐嗎？—會的，我會。

be動詞的疑問句也跟一般動詞一樣。由於be動詞的原形是「be」，所以是形式是《will+主詞+be…？》。

free
[fri]

形 空閒的；免費

Will you be free tomorrow?—Yes, I will.
你明天有空嗎？—有，我有空。

afternoon
[,æftɚ'nun]

名 下午

Will he be on time this afternoon?—No, he won't.
他這個下午會準時到嗎？—不，他不會。

in
[ɪn]

介 在～內

Will you be here in time?—Yes, I will.
你會及時到這裡來嗎？—會的，我會。

able
[ˈebl̩]

形 能夠

Will Mary be able to see him off on Sunday?—Yes, she will.
瑪莉星期天可以去送機嗎？—是的，她可以的。

nice
[naɪs]

形 好的

Will you be nice to your sister?—Yes, I will.
你會好好對待妹妹嗎？—是，我會的。

19.未來式（7）

1-17

句型《will you…》在此並不是「你會…嗎？」的意思，而是「可以幫我…嗎？」的意思，是一種委婉的請求。回答的方式也很多。

door
[dor]

名 門

Will you shut the door? —Sure.
可以麻煩你關門嗎？—沒問題。

quiet
[ˈkwaɪət]

形 安靜的

Will you please be quiet?—Sorry.
可否請你安靜一點？—對不起。

carry
[ˈkærɪ]

動 帶

Will you carry my groceries?—Yes, I will.
可否請你幫我拿我買的雜貨？—好的，我幫你。

sorry
[ˈsɔrɪ]

形 對不起

Will you mow the yard?—I'm sorry, I can't.
可否請你把院子的草割一割？—對不起我沒辦法。

garbage
[ˈgɑrbɪdʒ]

名 垃圾

Will you take out the garbage?—All right.
可否請你把垃圾拿出去倒掉？—可以啊！

句型《will you…》也有勸誘對方，「要不要做…」的意思。回答的時候，要看當時的情況喔！

video
['vɪdɪo]
名 錄影帶
Will you watch the video with us? —Yes, I will.
要不要和我們一起看錄影帶？—好啊！我要。

about
[ə'baʊt]
介 關於
Will you talk about your hobbies? —Yes, I will.
要不要聊聊你的興趣？—好啊！我要。

for
[fɔr]
介 為～
Will you sing the song for me? —No, I won't.
要不要為我唱這首歌？—不，我不要。

please
[pliz]
嘆 請
Will you have some coffee?—Yes, please.
來杯咖啡如何？—好的，麻煩了。

market
['markɪt]
名 市場
Will we go to the market, Tom?—Yes, let's go.
湯姆，我們去市場吧！—好，我們走吧。

21.助動詞—can, may等（1）

放在動詞的前面，來幫助動詞表達更廣泛意義的詞叫「助動詞」。助動詞的後面，一定要接原形動詞。助動詞can有：（1）表示「可能」、「有能力」的意思，相當於「會…」；（2）表示「許可」的意思，相當於「可以…」。

without
[wɪð'aʊt]
介 沒有～
I can live without you.
我沒有你也能活。

knife
[naɪf]
名 刀子
She can use the knife well.
她很會使用刀子。

can (could)
[kæn]

助 能；會
You can call me Mary.
您叫我瑪莉就行了。

really
['riəlɪ]

副 真的
You can use the car, really.
你可以用這車子，真的。

drive
[draɪv]

動 開車
Mary can drive a car.
瑪莉會開車。

22.助動詞─can, may等（2）

1-18

助動詞may有：（1）表示「許可」的意思，相當於「可以…」；
（2）表示「推測」的意思，相當於「可能…」。

around
[ə'raʊnd]

副 到處
You may look around.
你可以四處看看。

Thursday
['θɝzde]

名 星期四
You may come next Thursday.
你可以下禮拜四過來。

weekend
['wik'ɛnd]

名 週末
You may watch TV on weekends.
週末的時候，你可以看電視。

umbrella
[ʌm'brɛlə]

名 雨傘
It may rain today. Take an umbrella with you.
今天可能會下雨。你帶把傘吧。

wet
[wɛt]

形 潮濕的
The towel may be wet.
那毛巾可能是溼的。

1-18

助動詞must有：（1）表示「義務」、「命令」、「必須」的意思，相當於「得…」；（2）表示「推測」的意思，相當於「一定…」。

mother (mom；mommy) [ˈmɑðɚ]	名 母親；媽媽 I must help my mother. 我得幫助我母親。
follow [ˈfɑlo]	動 遵守；跟隨 You must follow the rules. 你必須遵守規則。
noise [nɔɪz]	名 噪音 They must not make noise. 他們不應該製造噪音。
crazy [krezɪ]	形 瘋狂的 I must be crazy! 我一定是瘋了！
lonely [ˈlonlɪ]	形 孤單 She must be very lonely. 她一定很寂寞。

1-18

助動詞should有表示「義務」的意思，語含勸對方最好做某事的口氣。相當於「應該…」、「最好…」。

keep [kip]	動 保持 We should keep our promises. 我們應該信守諾言。
honest [ˈɑnɪst]	形 誠實 You should be honest. 你應該要誠實。

hurry
['hɝɪ]

副 趕快
You should hurry up.
你應該加緊速度。

share
[ʃɛr]

動 分享
You should share your toys with others.
你應該跟別人分享你的玩具。

do (does，did，done)
[du]

動 做
You should do the right thing.
你應該做對的事情。

25.助動詞─否定句（1）

1-19

助動詞的後面接not就變成否定式，can的後面接not表示「不會…」、「不可能…」、「不可以…」的意思，可縮寫成 can't或是cannot。

basketball
['bæskɪtbɔl]

名 籃球
I cannot play basketball.
我不會打棒球。

paint
[pent]

動 繪畫
I can't paint.
我不會畫畫。

eighteen
['etin]

名 十八
He can't be only eighteen years old.
他不可能才十八歲。

already
[ɔl'rɛdɪ]

副 已經
You can't be hungry already.
你不可能已經餓了。

again
[ə'gen]

副 再次
You can't do that again.
你絕不可以再那麼做了。

1-19

may not是「可能不…」、「不可以…」，must not是「不可以…」的意思。must not比may not有更強的「禁止」的語意。

notice ['notɪs]	動 注意 He may not notice. 他可能不會注意到。
true [tru]	形 真的 It may not be true. 這可能不是真的。
camp [kæmp]	名 營隊；動 露營 You may not go camping tomorrow. 你明天不可以去露營。
bee [bi]	名 蜜蜂 You must not touch that bee. 你不可以碰那隻蜜蜂。
enter ['ɛntɚ]	動 進入 They must not enter my room. 他們不可以進我的房間。

27.助動詞─疑問句（1）

1-19

can的疑問句，是把can放在主詞的前面，變成《Can+主詞+動詞原形…?》的形式。意思相當於「會…嗎？」。回答「是」用《Yes, +代名詞+can》；回答「不是」用《No, +代名詞+can't》。

ride [raɪd]	名 乘車（馬）；動 騎，乘坐 Can you ride a horse? —No, I can't. 你會騎馬嗎？—不，我不會騎。
chopsticks ['tʃɑpˌstɪks]	名 筷子 Can you use chopsticks?—Yes, I can. 你會使用筷子嗎？—是，我會用。

lamp
[læmp]

名 燈

Can you fix the lamp?—No, I can't.
你會修檯燈嗎？—不，我不會。

remember
[rɪ'mɛmbɚ]

動 記得

Can you remember anything?—No, I can't.
你能記得任何事嗎？—不，我不記得了。

tree
[tri]

名 樹

Can you see that tree?—Yes, I can.
你看得到那棵樹嗎？—是，我看得到。

28.助動詞—疑問句（2）

1-19

may（可以）或must（必須）的疑問句，跟can一樣是《助動詞+主語+動詞原形…？》。

sit
[sɪt]

動 坐

May I sit down?—Sure.
我可以坐下嗎？—當然可以。

e-mail
[mel]

名 電子郵件

May I send an e-mail?—Yes, of course.
我可以寄封電子郵件嗎？—沒問題。

open
['opən]

動 打開

May I open the window?—No, you may not.
我可以打開窗戶嗎？—不，你不可以。

bag
[bæg]

名 袋子

Must I carry the bag?—Yes, you must.
我一定要帶這個包包嗎？—是的，你要。

need
[nid]

動 需要

Must Dolly have an operation?—No, she doesn't need to.
桃莉一定要開刀嗎？—不，她不需要。

1-20

be動詞還有表示「存在」的意思，相當於「在」、「有」等意思。

on [ɑn]	介 在～上面 The book is on the table. 書在桌上。
at [æt]	介 在～地點 John is at home. 約翰在家。
we (us，our， ours，ourselves) [wi]	代 我們（我們的，我們自己） We are in the car. 我們都在車裡。
playground ['ple͵graʊnd]	名 運動場 The children are on the playground 孩子們都在運動場。
I (me，my， mine，myself) [aɪ]	代 我（我，我的，我自己） I was there last night. 我昨晚在那裡。

1-20

表示「在」、「有」的意思時，否定句跟疑問句的形式，跟be動詞是一樣的。

card [kɑrd]	名 卡片 The card is not on the table. 卡片不在桌上。
bathroom ['bæθ͵rum]	名 浴室；盥洗室 John is not in the bathroom. 約翰不在浴室。

airport
['ɛr,port]

名 飛機場
They were not at the airport.
他們當時不在機場。

beach
[bitʃ]

名 海灘
Is he at the beach?—Yes, he is.
他在海邊嗎?—是呀,他在。

America
[ə'mɛrɪkə]

名 美國
Am I in America?—Yes, you are.
我在美國嗎?—對呀,你在。

31. be動詞的另一個意思—「有」(1)

1-20

there原本是「那裡」的意思,但是「there+be動詞」還有表示存在之意,相當於中文的「有(在)…」。單數時用《There is…》;複數時用《There are…》。

orange
['ɔrɪndʒ]

名 柳橙
There is an orange in the basket.
籃子裡有顆橘子。

milk
[mɪlk]

名 牛奶
There is a little milk in the glass.
玻璃杯裡有些牛奶。

class
[klæs]

名 班級
There are twenty girls in my class.
我們班有二十個女生。

hill
[hɪl]

名 小山
There are too many hills here.
這兒有太多山坡。

shop
[ʃɑp]

名 商店;動 購物
There were many shops in Michigan.
密西根州有很多商店。

32.be動詞的另一個意思—「有」（2）

否定句是在be動詞的後面接not，疑問句要把be動詞放在句首，變成《Is there…？》的形式。

clock
[klɑk]
名 時鐘
There isn't a clock in my room.
我房裡沒有時鐘。

black
[blæk]
形 黑色的
There isn't a black car by the gate.
門旁邊沒有黑色的車子。

classroom
['klæsrum]
名 教室
There isn't a piano in the classroom.
教室裡沒有鋼琴。

chalk
[tʃɔk]
名 粉筆
Is there chalk on the table?
桌上有粉筆嗎？

cookie
['kʊkɪ]
名 餅乾
Are there any cookies in the box?
盒子裡有餅乾嗎？

1.名詞的複數形（1）

我們常說二個以上要加s，這是英語的特色。英語中人或物是很清楚地分為一個（單數）跟二個以上（複數）的。人或物是複數時，名詞要用「複數形」。一般複數形要在詞尾加上-s。

spring
[sprɪŋ]
名 春天
Many plants come alive in spring.
很多植物在春天都會活起來。

eighty
['etɪ]
名 八十
I got eighty points.
我得了八十分。

50

cap [kæp]	名 帽子 I have four baseball caps. 我有四頂棒球帽。
two [tu]	名 二 I have two notebooks. 我有兩本筆記本。
three [θri]	名 三 Mr. Brown has three children. 布朗先生有三個小孩。

2.名詞的複數形（2）

1-21

把單複數弄清楚，說起英語會更道地喔！名詞的詞尾是ch, sh, s, x, o 時，複數形要加-es。

sandwich ['sænwɪtʃ]	名 三明治 He ate three sandwiches. 他吃了三個三明治。
break [brek]	動 打破 Dad broke five dishes. 爸爸打破了五個盤子。
collect [kə'lɛkt]	動 收集 Sam collects pictures of foxes. 山姆收集狐狸的照片。
box [bɑks]	名 盒子 There are three big boxes. 那裡有三個大盒子。
six [sɪks]	名 六 I have six potatoes. 我有六個馬鈴薯。

3.名詞的複數形（3）

詞尾是「子音+y」時，y要變成i，然後加-es。這裡的-es發音是[z]。

sleep [slip]	動 睡覺 The babies are sleeping. 寶寶們正熟睡著。
maybe [ˈmebi]	副 可能；也許 Maybe I know those ladies. 我可能認識那些女士。
five [faɪv]	名 五 We saw five flies. 我們看到五隻蒼蠅。
toy [tɔɪ]	名 玩具 The toy needs batteries. 這件玩具需要電池。
country [ˈkʌntrɪ]	名 國家 America and Canada are big countries. 美國跟加拿大是大國家。

4.名詞的複數形（4）

名詞的複數形也有不規則的變化，如man跟men（男人）、foot跟feet（腳）、mouse跟mice（老鼠）。也有單數跟複數是一樣的如sheep（羊）、deer（鹿）跟fish（魚）。

tooth [tuθ]	名 牙齒 He has five bad teeth. 他有五顆不好的牙。
mouse [maʊs]	名 老鼠；滑鼠 There are three mice. 有三隻老鼠。

woman ['wʊmən]	名 女士；女人 Do you know the women? 你認識那些女人嗎？
fish [fɪʃ]	動 釣魚；名 魚 I want to buy two fish. 我想買兩條魚。
sheep [ʃip]	名 綿羊 Are there many sheep in the field? 草原上有很多羊嗎？

5.可數名詞跟不可數名詞（1）

1-22

名詞大分為「可數名詞」跟「不可數名詞」兩類。可數名詞複數（2人或2個以上）時，要用複數形。另外，單數（1人、1個）時，前面常接a或an。

camera ['kæmərə]	名 照相機 I have a camera. 我有一台相機。
apple ['æpl̩]	名 蘋果 She gave me an apple. 她給了我一顆蘋果。
banana [bə'nænə]	名 香蕉 I have a banana and an apple. 我有一根香蕉跟一顆蘋果。
sport [spɔrt]	名 運動 Swimming is a good sport. 游泳是個好運動。
good [gʊd]	形 美好的 They are my good friends. 他們是我的好朋友。

小專欄

不可數名詞一般不接表示「單數的」a或an，也沒有複數形。不可數名詞基本上有下列三種。

1.固有名詞（唯一的，大寫開頭的人名、地名等）
2.物質名詞（沒有一定形狀的空氣、水、麵包等）
3.抽象名詞（性質、狀態籠統，無形的愛、美、和平、音樂等）

4.固有名詞（人名、地名等）

I live in Paris.
我住在巴黎。

2.物質名詞（空氣、水、麵包等）

I want a glass of water.
我想一杯水。

3.抽象名詞（愛、美、和平、音樂等）

We love peace.
我喜歡和平。

6.可數名詞跟不可數名詞（2）

1-22

不能用1個、2個來計算的名詞，也可以用表示「量」的形容詞，來表示「多或少」。如：some（一些），much（很多），little（很少），a little（一點點），no（沒有），a great deal of（很多），a lot of（很多）…。

juice [dʒus]	名 果汁 I want some apple juice. 我想要一點蘋果汁。
food [fud]	名 食物 I need a lot of food. 我需要很多食物。

salad
['sæləd]

名 沙拉；涼拌生菜
I would like some salad.
我想要一些沙拉。

money
['mʌnɪ]

名 錢
She has no money.
她沒有錢。

clothes
[kloðz]

名 衣服
He has a great deal of clothes.
他有很多衣服。

7.可數名詞跟不可數名詞（3）

1-23

不可數名詞在當作單位名詞時，有時變成可數的。

glass
[glæs]

名 玻璃杯
I want two glasses of milk.
我要兩杯牛奶。

cup
[kʌp]

名 杯子
Give me a cup of coffee.
給我一杯咖啡。

bread
[brɛd]

名 麵包
She has a slice of bread.
她吃一片麵包。

paper
['pepɚ]

名 紙；報紙
There is a sheet of paper.
那裡有一張紙。

fresh
[frɛʃ]

形 淡水的；新鮮的
Would you like a glass of fresh juice?
你要不要來一杯新鮮的果汁？

8.指示代名詞（1）

指示眼睛可以看到的東西或人叫「指示代名詞」。指近處的東西或人，單數用this（這個），複數形用 these（這些）。

eraser
[ɪˈrezɚ]

名 橡皮擦
This is my eraser.
這是我的橡皮擦。

plan
[plæn]

名 計畫
This is a great plan.
這計畫很棒。

seat
[sit]

名 座位
These seats are taken .
這些位子有人坐了。

surprise
[səˈpraɪz]

名 驚奇
This is a big surprise!
這是個大大的驚喜!

these
[ðiz]

代 這些；形 這些
Are these your magazines?
這些是你的雜誌嗎？

9.指示代名詞（2）

指示較為遠處的人或物，單數用that（那個），複數用those（那些）。

father (dad；daddy)
[ˈfɑðɚ]

名 父親；爸爸
That is my father.
那位是我的父親。

coat
[kot]

名 外套
That is your coat.
那是你的外套。

large [lɑrdʒ]	形 大的 That's a large sweater! 那真是件大毛衣！
movie ['muvɪ]	名 電影 That was the best movie of the year! 那是年度的最佳電影！
same [sem]	形 一樣的 Those books are the same. 那些書都是一樣的。

10.指示代名詞（3）

1-24

this從「這個」的意思，發展成「（介紹人說的）這位是…」、「這裡是…」、「今天是…」及「（打電話指自己）我是…」的意思。

second ['sɛkənd]	形 第二的 This is George, my second cousin. 這是我第二個表兄弟，喬治。
national ['nɛʃənl̩]	名 國家 This is the national theater. 這是國家劇院。
nephew ['nɛfju]	名 姪兒，外甥 This is my nephew. 這位是我外甥。
kitchen ['kɪtʃən]	名 廚房 This is the kitchen. 這裡是廚房。
hello [hə'lo]	嘆 你好 Hello, this is Ann. 你好！我是安。〈打電話時〉

指示眼前較為遠處的事物的 that，也表示「那、那件事」的意思。

special
['spɛʃəl]

形 特別的
That's a special gift.
這是個特別的禮物。

third
[θɜd]

形 第三的
That's her third book.
那是她的第三本書。

department store
[ɪ'rezɚ]

名 百貨公司
That is a huge department store.
這家百貨公司真大。

idea
[aɪ'dɪə]

名 主意
That's a good idea.
那真是個好主意。

question
['kwɛstʃən]

名 問題
That's an interesting question.
這是個有趣的問題。

12.名詞及代名詞的所有格—表示「的」的詞（1）

1-24

表示「…的」的形式的叫「所有格」。表示人或動物的名詞，以接
《…'s》表示所有格。

red
[rɛd]

形 紅色的
My father's car is red.
我父親的車子是紅色的。

name
[nem]

名 名字
The dog's name is Kant.
這隻狗的名字叫康德。

dictionary [ˈdɪkʃənˌɛrɪ]	名 字典 That is my brother's dictionary. 那是我哥哥的字典。
near [nɪr]	介 在～附近 My uncle's house is near the station. 我叔叔的家離車站很近。
before [bɪˈfor]	副 以前 Have you seen Anna's brother before? 你以前看過安娜的弟弟嗎？

13.名詞及代名詞的所有格─表示「的」的詞（2）

1-25

表示人或動動以外，無生命物的名詞，一般用《of…》的形式來表示所有格。of…修飾前面的名詞。

leg [lɛg]	名 腿 We broke the legs of the desk. 我們弄壞了桌腳。
south [saʊθ]	名 南方 It is raining hard in the south of Taiwan. 台灣南部正下著大雨。
autumn (fall) [ˈɔtəm]	名 秋天 Autumn is the best season of the year. 秋天是一年中最棒的季節。
leader [ˈlidɚ]	名 領導人 He was the leader of his class. 他是班上的領導者。
January [ˈdʒænjʊˌɛrɪ]	名 一月 January is the first month of the year. 一月是一年當中的第一個月。

14.名詞及代名詞的所有格—表示「的」的詞（3）

人稱代名詞的所有格，各有固定的形式。《I→my〔our〕》、《you→your〔your〕》、《he→his〔their〕》、《she→her〔their〕》、《it→its〔their〕》。〔 〕裡是複數。

classmate
['klæsmet]

名 （同班）同學
John is my classmate.
約翰是我的同學。

grandfather (grandpa)
['grænd,faðə]

名 祖父；爺爺
He is my grandfather.
他是我的祖父。

out
[aʊt]

副 出去
She goes out with her friends.
她和她的朋友出去。

English
['ɪŋglɪʃ]

名 英語
They speak English in their country.
他們在他們的國家裡說英語。

head
[hɛd]

名 頭
The dog is shaking its head.
那隻狗搖著牠的頭。

15.名詞及代名詞的所有格—表示「的」的詞（4）

指示代名詞的 this, that等，也可以當作指示形容詞，來表示「…的」的意思。但可不是「所有格」喔！

simple
['sɪmpl]

形 簡單
That question was simple.
那個題目很簡單。

truck
[trʌk]

名 卡車
Who drives that truck?
是誰開那輛卡車的？

king
[kɪŋ]

名 國王
You are not the king of this country.
你不是這個國家的國王。

all
[ɔl]

代 全部
Did you buy all of those pens?
那些筆全是你買的嗎？

during
['djʊrɪŋ]

介 在～的時候
What have you been doing during these days?
這些日子你都在做些什麼？

16.所有代名詞跟反身代名詞（1）

1-26

表示「…的東西」的代名詞叫「所有代名詞」，這個用法是為了不重複同一名詞。所指的「物」不管是單數或複數，所有代名詞都是一樣。所有代名詞1個字等同於〈所有格＋名詞〉。

picture
['pɪktʃɚ]

名 照片
That picture is hers.
那張照片是她的。

sir
[sɝ]

名 先生
These bags are yours, sir.
這些包包是你的，先生。

television (TV)
['tɛlə,vɪʒən]

名 電視
The television is ours.
這電視是我們的。

boat
[bot]

動 乘船；名 船
The boat is his.
這艘船是他的。

farm
[fɑrm]

名 農場
The farm is not yours. It's theirs.
這農場不是你的，是他們的。

下面的相同意思，不同的說法，是考試常出現的，要多注意喔！

That is our car.
那是我們的車。
↓
That car is ours.
那車是我們的。

These are my pens.
這些是我的筆。
↓
These pens are mine.
這些筆是我的。

That is Smith's ball.
那是史密斯的球。
↓
That ball is Smith's.
那個球是史密斯的。

17.所有代名詞跟反身代名詞（2）

1-26

動詞的受詞等，跟句子的主詞是一樣的時候，要用表示「自己…」的特別的代名詞，叫「反身代名詞」。也就是人稱代名詞加上 -self（單數形）, -selves（複數形）。

ask
[æsk]
動 問
I asked myself.
我問我自己。

believe
[bɪˈliv]
動 相信
You should believe in yourself.
你應該相信自己。

hurt [hɝt]	動 傷害；受傷 The man hurt himself. 這個人傷了他自己。
prepare [prɪˈpɛr]	動 準備 My friends prepared for the party by themselves. 我的朋友們自己準備了派對。
often [ˈɔfən]	副 通常 My sister and I often cook dinner for ourselves. 我姊姊和我通常都自己作晚餐。

18.所有代名詞跟反身代名詞（3）

1-26

反身代名詞也有強調主詞的作用。

make [mek]	動 做；製造 I made the cake myself. 我親手做了一個蛋糕。
wash [waʃ]	動 清洗 I washed all the dishes myself. 我自己洗了所有的碗盤。
pay [pe]	動 付（錢） He paid the bill himself. 他自己付了帳單。
pick [pɪk]	副 拿起；挑選 She picked the new house herself. 她自己一個人挑選了新家。
party [ˈpɑrtɪ]	名 派對 They prepared for the party themselves. 他們自己準備了派對。

19.不定代名詞—some, any等（1）

沒有特定的指某人或某物的代名詞叫「不定代名詞」。不定代名詞的 some 含糊的指示人或物的數量，表示「一些、幾個」的意思。

basket
['bæskɪt']
名 籃子
There are some apples in the basket.
籃子裡有一些蘋果。

lemon
['lɛmən]
名 檸檬
Give me some lemons, please.
請給我一些檸檬。

tea
[ti]
名 茶
I want some tea.
我要一些茶。

every
['ɛvrɪ]
形 每個
I buy some books every month.
我每個月都買幾本書。

test
[tɛst]
名 測驗小考
Some of the test questions were too hard.
這個考試中的部份題目真的太難了。

20.不定代名詞—some, any等（2）

something表示「某事物」，somebody, someone表示「某人」、「誰」的意思。這些都是單數。

smell
[smɛl]
動 聞起來
I smell something.
我聞到某種味道。

something
['sʌm,θɪŋ]
代 某些（事情、物品）
I have something to tell you.
有話要跟你說。

look
[lʊk]

動 看

There's something I want you to look at.
這裡有些東西我想給你看。

wake
[wek]

動 醒來

Somebody has to wake me up.
要有個人叫我起床。

someone (somebody)
[ˈsʌmˌwʌn]

代 某人

There is someone at the door.
門旁有個人。

21.不定代名詞—some, any等（3）

1-27

疑問句中表示「多少個」、「多少」、「多少人」時，用 any。否定句用 not…any，意思是「一個也（一人也）…沒有」。

wish
[wɪʃ]

名 願望；希望

Do you have any wishes?
你有任何願望嗎？

hot dog
[ˈhɑtˌdɔg]

名 熱狗

Do you want any hot dogs?
你要不要熱狗？

news
[njuz]

名 新聞

Is there any big news today?
今天有什麼大新聞嗎?

kid
[ˈkɪd]

名 小孩；小兒

I don't have any kids.
我沒有小孩。

Ms.
[mɪz]

名 小姐

Ms. Jolie doesn't have any friends.
裘莉小姐沒有任何朋友。

同樣地，在疑問句跟否定句中 anything是「什麼」、「什麼也」的意思；anybody, anyone是「有誰」、「誰也」的意思。

pollution
[pə'luʃən]

名 污染
I don't know anything about the pollution.
污染的事我什麼也不知道。

but
[bʌt]

連 但是
They are busy, but I don't have anything to do.
他們在忙，但我沒什麼事可以做。

well
[wɛl]

嘆 嗯
Well, I don't see anyone here!
嗯，我在這裡連個人影都沒看見!

hamburger
['hæmbɝgɚ]

名 漢堡
Anybody can make a hamburger.
不管誰都會做漢堡。

grow
[gro]

動 種植
Does anybody grow flowers at home?
這裡有誰在家裡有種花嗎？

all是「全部」，each是「各個」的意思。其中《all of+複數名詞》被當作複數，《all of+不可數名詞》被當作單數，而 each則都是當作單數。

of
[əv]

介 ～的
I know all of them.
我認識他們所有人。

agree
[ə'gri]

動 同意
All of us agreed to do that.
我們全都同意這麼做。

66

play [ple]	動 玩；演戲 All of us can play cards. 我們全都會玩牌。
each [itʃ]	形 各個 Each of us has a car. 我們每人都有車。
cell phone [ˈsɛlˌfon]	名 手機 Each of the girls has a cell phone. （他們之中）每一位女生都有手機。

24.不定代名詞─all, each等（2）

1-28

both跟 either都是用在形容二個事物的時候，但是 both表示「兩者都」，被當作複數，either則表示「兩者中任一」，被當作單數。

may (might) [maɪt]	助 可能 Both of you may go. 你們兩個都得離開。
fine [faɪn]	形 好 Both my parents are fine. 我父母兩人都很好。
appear [əˈpɪr]	動 出現 Both of them appeared at the party. 他們都在派對上出現了。
team [tim]	名 隊伍；團隊 Either of the teams will win. 那兩隊其中之一會贏。
pencil [ˈpɛnsl]	名 鉛筆 Write either with a pen or with a pencil. 用原子筆或鉛筆寫都可以。

one除了「一個、一個的」意思以外，還可以用來避免重複，代替前面出現過的名詞。不定代名詞 one 跟前面的名詞相對應，表示跟前面的名詞是「同類的東西」，常用於《a+形容詞+ one》的句型。

dirty
[ˈdɝtɪ]

形 骯髒的
This cup is dirty, I need a clean one.
這片杯子很髒，我需要一個乾淨的。

sweater
[ˈswɛtɚ]

名 毛衣
Do you have a sweater?—Yes, I have one.
你有毛衣嗎？—有，我有一件。

motorcycle
[ˈmotɚˌsaɪkl]

名 摩托車
He has a motorcycle. I want one, too.
他有一台摩托車，我也想要有一台。

small
[smɔl]

形 小的
Do you want a big apple or a small one?
你要大的蘋果還是要小的？

give
[gɪv]

動 給
We could give her this old TV and buy a new one.
我們可以把這台舊電視給她，然後買一台新的。

26.不定代名詞—all, each等（4）

another表示不定的「又一個東西（人）」、「另一個東西（人）」。another其實是由〈an+ other〉來的，至於the other則表示特定的「（兩個當中的）另一個東西（人）」。

show
[ʃo]

動 表演；展示
I don't like this one. Show me another.
我不喜歡這個。給我看看別的。

another
[əˈnʌðɚ]

形 另一的
Do you want another cup of coffee?
你要不要再來一杯咖啡？

piece
[pis]

名 碎片
Will you have another piece of cake?
再來一片蛋糕如何？

egg
[ɛg]

名 蛋
This egg is bigger than the other.
這顆蛋比另一顆大。

side
[saɪd]

名 邊
He lives on the other side of the river.
他住在河的另一邊。

27.名詞其它該注意的用法─it, they等（1）

1-29

it除了指前接的「特定的東西」以外，也含糊地指「天氣」、「時間」、「距離」跟「明暗」等。

today
[tə'de]

名 今天
It's fine today.
今天天氣好。

outside
['aʊt'saɪd]

介 在～外面
It's cold outside.
外面很冷。

thirty
['θɝtɪ]

名 三十
It's seven-thirty.
現在七點三十分。

twelve
[twɛlv]

名 十二
It's about twelve kilometers away.
大概有十二公里遠。

dark
[dɑrk]

名 黑暗
It's getting dark outside.
外面漸漸變暗了。

28.名詞其它該注意的用法─it, they等（2）

it也可以放在句首，對應後面的不定詞（to＋原形動詞）。

answer [ˈænsɚ]	動 回答；答覆 It is easy to answer this question. 回答這個問題很簡單。
spell [spɛl]	動 拼字 It is difficult to spell the word. 要拼出這個單字很困難。
boring [ˈborɪŋ]	形 令人感到乏味的 It is boring to stay at home all day. 待在家裡一整天是件很無聊的事。
foreign [ˈfɔrɪn]	形 外國的 It is exciting to travel to a foreign country. 到異國旅遊是件興奮的事。
Internet [ˈɪntɚ͵nɛt]	名 網際網路 It is interesting to chat on the Internet. 在網路上聊天是件有趣的事。

29.名詞其它該注意的用法─it, they等（3）

we, you, they也有含糊的指「一般的人，人們，相關的人」的用法。翻譯的時候可以配合前後文。

anything [ˈɛnɪ͵θɪŋ]	代 任何東西 We shouldn't take anything that is not ours. 我們不該拿不屬於自己的東西。
blind [blaɪnd]	形 盲的 Love makes you blind. 愛情使你盲目。

as
[æz]

介 當作

Take your pain as a challenge.
把你的痛苦當作挑戰。

from
[frʌm]

介 來自於

You can see Jade Mountain from here.
從這裡可以看到玉山。

rich
[rɪtʃ]

形 富有

They say he is very rich.
據說他很有錢。

30.名詞其它該注意的用法─it, they等（4）

1-30

含有代名詞的片語，也要多注意喔！像是each other（互相）,one another（互相）,one after another（一個接著一個）等，都相當實用。

monthly
[ˈmʌnθlɪ]

形 每個月的；副 每月；名 月刊

We call each other monthly.
我們每個月彼此互通電話。

minute
[ˈmɪnɪt]

名 分鐘

They hug each other for a couple of minutes.
他們抱著對方持續幾分鐘。

finally
[ˈfaɪnəlɪ]

副 最後的

They looked at one another and finally laughed.
她們看著彼此，然後終於笑了出來。

die
[daɪ]

動 死

The soldiers died one after another.
士兵們一個接著一個死了。

other
[ˈʌðɚ]

形 其他的

We will never forget one another.
我們絕不會忘記彼此的。

1.a跟the（1）

冠詞是一種形容詞，特定指單數的「一個東西」、「一個人」時，名詞前面要接冠詞 a（an）。但是 a只用在不限定的人或物上，「限定的」人或物就要用「Point2」的冠詞 the。所以 a叫「不定冠詞」，the叫「定冠詞」

elementary school
[ɛlə'mɛntərɪ,skul]

名 小學；國小
There's an elementary school near my house
我家附近有一所小學。

Mrs.
['mɪsɪz]

名 太太；夫人
Mrs. Green is a doctor.
格林夫人是個醫生。

line
[laɪn]

名 行；列
Please stand in a line.
請站成一直線。

evening
['ivnɪŋ]

名 傍晚
This is a wonderful evening.
這真是個美好的黃昏。

elephant
['ɛləfənt]

名 大象
There is a huge elephant!
那裡有一隻好大的大象!

2.a跟the（2）

在彼此都知道的情況下，指示同類事物中的某一個，也就是指示「特定的」人或物時，名詞前面要接 the，表示「那個…」的意思。

nine
[naɪn]

名 九
The movies starts at nine.
那齣電影九點開演。

blackboard
['blækbord]

名 黑板
Write the answer on the blackboard.
把答案寫在黑板上。

page
[pedʒ]

名 頁
Please turn to page twenty of the book.
請翻到這本書的第二十頁。

restaurant
[ˈrɛstərənt]

名 餐廳
They're waiting for us at the restaurant now.
他們正在那間餐廳等我們。

close
[klos]

動 關閉
Please close the door.
請關門。

3.a跟the（3）

1-31

不定冠詞 a是用在不限定的單數名詞前面，所以複數名詞或不可數名詞不用加 a。

cat
[kæt]

名 貓
I don't like cats.
我不喜歡貓。

mistake
[məˈstek]

名 錯誤
I made some mistakes.
我犯了些錯誤。

headache
[ˈhɛdˌek]

名 頭痛
I often get headaches.
我常有頭痛的毛病。

life
[laɪf]

名 生活
She enjoys life.
她享受生活。

morning
[ˈmɔrnɪŋ]

名 早晨
They drink coffee in the morning.
他們早上喝咖啡。

4.a跟the（4）

只要是指「特定的」人或物，不管是複數名詞或不可數名詞，都用the。

station
['steʃən]

名 車站
I saw the girls at the bus station.
我在公車站看到那些女孩。

grass
[græs]

名 草
I lay on the grass.
我躺在草地上。

salt
[sɔlt]

名 鹽
Please pass the salt.
請把鹽遞給我。

water
['wɑtɚ]

名 水
I jump into the water.
我跳進水裡。

let
[lɛt]

動 讓；允許
Let her have the money.
讓她拿那些錢吧。

5.a跟the該注意的用法（1）

a的後面接上「單位」，也有表示「每…」的意思。

hour
[aʊr]

名 小時
He studies six hours a day.
他一天讀書六小時。

museum
[mju'ziəm]

名 博物館
We go to the museum once a month.
我們每個月去博物館一次。

menu
['mɛnju]

名 菜單
They change their menu twice a year.
他們每年會換兩次菜單。

supermarket
['supɚˌmarkɪt]

名 超級市場
I have to go to the supermarket once a month.
我每個月必須要去超市一次。

year
[jɪr]

名 年
They go to Japan once a year.
他們每年去一趟日本。

6.a跟the該注意的用法（2）

1-32

a也有表示「同種類的全體」的意思，也就是總稱的用法。

rabbit
['ræbɪt]

名 兔子
A rabbit has long ears.
兔子有長長的耳朵。

neck
[nɛk]

名 脖子
A giraffe has a long neck.
長頸鹿的有長長的脖子。

dream
[drim]

名 夢；夢想
A dream needs hard work.
夢想需要努力

vacation
[vəˈkeʃən]

名 假期
A vacation refreshes your mind.
假期滋養人的心靈。

bird
[bɝd]

名 鳥
Birds of a feather flock together.
物以類聚。

7.a跟the該注意的用法（3）

the也用在自然地被「特定」的東西之前，如「月亮」或「太陽」等獨一無二的自然物。還有only（只有一個）、first（最初）、second（第二）等附有形容詞的名詞前。

east
[ist]

名 東方
The Sun rises in the east.
太陽從東方升起。

moon
[mun]

名 月亮
The Moon goes around the Earth.
月亮繞著地球轉。

Sun
[sʌn]

名 太陽
The Earth goes around the Sun.
地球繞著太陽轉。

painting
[ˈpentɪŋ]

名 繪畫
Look! That's the best painting of DaVinci.
你看！那是達文西最好的一幅畫。

first
[fɝst]

副 先；第一
He won first prize.
他得了第一名。

8.a跟the該注意的用法（4）

同樣地，從說話者跟聽話者當時的情況，自然而然地被「特定」的事物，也用the。也就是從周圍的狀況，知道對方指的是什麼。

pass
[pæs]

動 通過
Pass the salt, please.
請把鹽傳過來。（指的當然是桌上的鹽）

tiger
[ˈtaɪgɚ]

名 老虎
Look at the tiger.
看那隻老虎。（因為彼此都看到了）

sound
[saʊnd]

名 聲音；動 聽起來
What was that sound?
那是什麼聲音呀？（因為彼此都聽到了）

sentence
[ˈsɛntəns]

名 句子
Explain this sentence to me, please.
請幫我解釋這個句子。

ticket
[ˈtɪkɪt]

名 票
Give me the ticket.
給我票。

9.冠詞跟習慣用法（1）

1-33

在英語的成語中，冠詞也有固定的用法，下面舉出的習慣用法，一般用 the。

Miss
[mɪs]

名 小姐
Miss Brown can play the violin.
伯朗小姐會拉小提琴。

radio
[ˈredɪˌo]

名 收音機
He listens to the radio in the morning.
他在早上聽收音機。

number
[ˈnʌmbɚ]

名 號碼；數字
By the way, may I have your phone number?
喔，順便一提，可以給我你的電話嗎？

postcard
[ˈpostˌkɑrd]

名 明信片
In the end, he still didn't get the postcard.
最後，他還是沒收到明信片。

moment
[ˈmomənt]

名 片刻
At that moment, she knew the truth.
在那一刻，她知道了真相。

10.冠詞跟習慣用法（2）

1-34

下面的成語要用a。

Saturday
['sætɚde]

名 星期六
Have a good time on Saturday!
星期六玩得開心點！

OK
['o'ke]

形 好；可以
Let's take a walk.—OK, let's go.
我們來散散步吧！—好啊，我們走吧。

helpful
['hɛlpfəl]

形 有益的
Let's take a break. It will be helpful.
我們休息一下吧。那會很有幫助的。

feel
[fil]

動 感覺
Take a deep breath and you will feel better.
深呼吸會讓你舒服點。

long
[lɔg]

形 長時間的
He has been in Hong Kong for a long time.
他在香港好一段時間了。

11.冠詞跟習慣用法（3）

1-34

慣用表現中，也有省略冠詞的情況。

foot
[fʊt]

名 腳
I go to school on foot.
我走路上學。

weak
[wik]

形 虛弱的
He is at home because he's weak now.
他在家，因為他現在很虛弱。

soon
[sun]

副 很快地
Dad will come back soon.
爸爸馬上會回來。

even
['ivən]

副 甚至
Kate can play guitar and even write songs.
凱特會彈吉他，甚至會寫歌。

school
[skul]

名 學校
Do you go to school on Sundays?
你星期天要上學嗎？

12.冠詞跟習慣用法（4）

1-34

「運動」、「三餐」、「學科」等相關敘述，一般是不加冠詞的。

forget
[fɚ'gɛt]

動 忘記
Let's forget about the test and play baseball!
我們忘了考試，來打棒球吧！

together
[tə'gɛðɚ]

副 一起
We have lunch together.
我們一起吃午餐。

Chinese
[tʃaɪ'niz]

名 中文
He majors in Chinese.
他主修中文。

joy
[dʒɔɪ]

名 喜樂
Irene likes science. It's such a joy for her.
艾琳喜歡科學。那對她來說真是種快樂。

summer
['sʌmɚ]

名 夏天
Pat doesn't like summer.
派特不喜歡夏天。

13.表示數跟量的形容詞—多.少（1）

「數」很多的時候用 many，「量」很多的時候用 much。many, much常用在疑問句跟否定句中。many後面要接的是可數事物，像是可以數出來的桌椅、車票…等；much是用來形容不可數的東西，像是水或果汁、很抽象的錢、時間…等。

room
[rum]
名 房間
There aren't many books in my room.
我房間裡沒有很多書。

bank
[bæŋk]
名 銀行
Are there many banks in your city?
你的城市裡有很多銀行嗎？

butter
[ˈbʌtɚ]
名 奶油
I don't want too much butter on my toast.
我的吐司不要太多奶油。

sugar
[ˈʃʊgɚ]
名 糖
How much sugar do you need?
你需要多少糖？

bottle
[ˈbɑtl]
名 瓶子
Is there much milk in the bottle?
瓶子裡有很多牛奶嗎？

14.表示數跟量的形容詞—多.少（2）

可以同時表示「數」跟「量」很多的是 a lot of。在疑問句跟否定句以外的一般肯定句中，a lot of比 many跟 much還要常使用。

rule
[rul]
名 規則
There are a lot of rules in this class.
這個班級有很多規則。

problem
[ˈprɑbləm]
名 問題
I have a lot of problems.
我碰到了很多問題。

want
[wɑnt]

動 要
They want a lot of water.
他想要很多水。

map
[mæp]

名 地圖
It was a lot of work to make a map.
做一張地圖費了好大功夫。

jeans
[dʒinz]

名 牛仔褲
Those jeans cost a lot of money.
那些牛仔褲花了我不少錢。

15.表示數跟量的形容詞—多・少（3）

1-35

表示「數」有一些時，用 a few，而且是用在複數形可數名詞上；表示「量」有一些時，用 a little，用在不可數名詞上。

few
[fju]

形 很少
I have a few friends.
我有2、3個朋友。

block
[blɑk]

名 區塊
It's only a few blocks away.
只不過幾條街過去而已。

magic
['mædʒɪk]

名 魔法
I know only a few magic tricks.
我只會一些魔術技法。

little
['lɪtl̩]

形 小的；有一點
I have a little money.
我有一些錢。

thirsty
['θɝstɪ]

形 口渴
They were thirsty and drank a little coffee.
他們口渴，於是喝了一些咖啡。

1-35

有冠詞 a的時候，含有肯定的「有一點」的語意。但是把 a拿掉只用 few, little，就含有「只有一點點」、「幾乎沒有」等否定意味。當然 few是用在「數」，而little用在「量」上。

past
[pæst]

名 過去

I had few friends in the past.
過去，我沒什麼朋友。

own
[on]

動 擁有

The kid owns few toys.
那小孩只擁有一點點玩具。

rest
[rɛst]

名 休息

They took a rest and drank a little water.
他們休息了一下並喝了一點水。

ice
[aɪs]

名 冰

There is little ice in the cup.
杯子裡幾乎沒什麼冰塊。

experience
[ɪk'spɪrɪəns]

名 經驗；動 體驗

I have little experience.
我沒什麼經驗。

17.表示數跟量的形容詞—some, any等（1）

1-36

數詞是用來表示數目的，其中有分「計算數量」跟「表示順序」的 兩種數詞。

sixteen
[sɪks'tin]

名 十六

Johnny has sixteen pens
強尼有十六支筆。

hundred
['hʌndrəd]

形 百

He has two hundred kinds of stamps.
他有200種郵票。

82

family
['fæmlɪ]

名 家庭;家人

He is the first son in his family.
他是家中的長男。

apartment
[ə'pɑrtmənt]

名 公寓

Our apartment is on the third floor.
我們的公寓在第三層樓。

December
[dɪ'sɛmbɚ]

名 十二月

December is the twelfth month of the year.
12月是一年中的第12個月。

18.表示數跟量的形容詞—some, any等(2)

1-36

表示「不特定的數或量」用 some,意思是「一些的」。中譯時有時候字面上是不翻譯的。

rice
[raɪs]

名 稻米;飯

I want some rice.
我想要一些飯。

key
[ki]

名 鑰匙

There are some keys in the box.
箱子裡有幾支鑰匙。

bring
[brɪŋ]

動 帶著

Bring me some water, please.
請拿一些水給我。

fruit
[frut]

名 水果

My mother went to buy some fruit.
我媽媽去買水果。

chance
[tʃæns]

名 機會

Consider it a chance to get some exercise.
當它是個運動的好機會。

19.表示數跟量的形容詞—some, any等（3）

通常在疑問句和否定句中，表示「不特定的數或量」時要用 any。

future ['fjutʃɚ]	名 未來 Do you have any plans for the future? 你對未來有什麼計劃嗎？
heart [hɑrt]	名 心；心臟 Do I have any problems with my heart? 我的心臟有什麼問題嗎？
interest ['ɪntrɪst]	名 興趣；嗜好 Do you have any interests? 你有什麼嗜好嗎？
mind [maɪnd]	名 心智 Do you have any ideas in mind? 你腦子裡有什麼點子嗎？
serious ['sɪrɪəs]	形 嚴重的 Are there any serious problems? 有什麼嚴重的問題嗎？

20.表示數跟量的形容詞—some, any等（4）

1-36

any跟否定的 not一起使用時，表示「一點…也沒有」的意思。當然「數」跟「量」都可以使用。

foreigner ['fɔrɪnɚ]	名 外國人 She doesn't know any foreigners. 她一個外國人也不認識。
ground [graʊnd]	名 地面 I don't see any trash on the ground. 我看不到地上任何有垃圾。

package
['pækɪdʒ]

名 包；包裝
I didn't see any books in the package.
我沒看見有任何書在包裹裡。

man
[mæn]

名 男人
Sarah doesn't want any advice from a man.
莎拉不想要從個男人那裡得到任何建議。

this
[ðɪs]

名 這個
I don't have any money left this month.
這個月我一毛錢也沒剩下。

21.副詞該注意的用法（1）

always（總是，經常）、often（常常，往往）、usually（通常）、sometimes（有時）、once（一次）等表示頻率的副詞，通常要放在一般動詞的前面，但是要放在 be動詞的後面。

seven
['sɛvən]

名 七
He always gets up at seven.
他總是七點起床。

noodle
['nudl̩]

名 麵條
I often cook noodles by myself.
我經常自己煮麵。

theater
['θiətɚ]

名 戲院
I often go to the theater alone.
我經常一個人去戲院。

bed
[bɛd]

名 床
I usually go to bed early.
平常我很早睡覺。

sometimes
['sʌmtaɪmz]

副 有時候
He is sometimes absent from school.
他有時會不去上學。

表示「程度」的副詞，通常要放在它修飾的形容詞或副詞的前面。但是要記住喔！同樣是程度副詞的 enough（足夠），可是要放在它修飾的形容詞或副詞的後面。我們來跟另一個程度副詞 very比較看看。

He is very tall.
他很高大。
↓
He is tall enough.
他夠高大了。

This beer is very cool.
這啤酒很冰。
↓
This beer is cool enough.
這啤酒已經夠冰了。

22.副詞該注意的用法（2）

1-37

修飾動詞表示「很」、「非常」的時候，一般用 very much。

enjoy
[ɪnˈdʒɔɪ]

動 喜愛
I enjoyed the music very much.
我非常享受音樂之美。

thank
[θæŋk]

名 謝謝
Thank you very much.
真的很謝謝你。

very [ˈvɛrɪ]	副 很;非常 I like the present very much. 我非常喜歡這個禮物。
too [tu]	副 也;太 I like strawberries very much, too. 我也很喜歡草莓。
he (him,his,himself) [hi]	代 他(他,他的,他自己) He likes tennis very much. 他非常喜歡打網球。

23.副詞該注意的用法(3)

1-37

only(僅,只)、even(甚至)也可以修飾名詞跟代名詞,放在名詞或代名詞的前面。

twice [twaɪs]	副 兩次,兩倍 She came only twice. 她只來過兩次。
one [wʌn]	名 一 It's only one o'clock. 現在才一點鐘。
learn [lɜn]	動 學習 It's the only way to learn. 這是學習的唯一方法。
wear [wɛr]	動 穿;戴 Jack even wears a raincoat. 傑克甚至穿了件雨衣。
officer [ˈɔfɪsɚ]	名 官員 Laura even called the police officer. 萊拉甚至打給了警察。

一般動詞（be動詞以外的動詞）裡面，也有後面要接「補語」的動詞。代表性的有 become（成為…）。

successful [sək'sɛsfəl]	形 成功的 She became a successful model. 她成為一個成功的模特兒。
become [bɪ'kʌm]	動 成為 He became a teacher. 他成為老師。
club [klʌb]	名 社團 Tom and I became the leaders of this club. 湯姆跟我變成這社團的領導人。
thin [θɪn]	形 瘦的 He became thin. 他變瘦了。
July [dʒu'laɪ]	名 七月 It becomes very hot in July. 七月變得很熱。

2.有補語的句子・有受詞的句子（2）

1-38

後接補語的動詞，有下面幾個，要記下來喔！這些動詞的補語，常常是形容詞。

great [gret]	形 很好 She looked great. 她看起來很棒。
several ['sɛvərəl]	形 數個 He went crazy after several months. 幾個月後他就瘋了。

clear
[klɪr]

形 清醒的

She grew old and does not have clear thinking.
她老了並且思考不清楚。

pretty
[ˈprɪtɪ]

副 相當

She seems pretty smart.
她似乎很聰明。

delicious
[dɪˈlɪʃəs]

形 美味的

It smells good! It must be delicious.
聞起來很香！它一定很好吃。

3.有補語的句子・有受詞的句子（3）

一般動詞中，動作會影響到他物的。也就是有受詞的，叫及物動詞；動作不影響到他物，沒有受詞的叫不及物動詞。

fourth
[forθ]

形 第四的

I had my fourth try.
我做了第四次的嘗試。

letter
[ˈlɛtɚ]

名 信件

I write her a letter.
我寫了一封信給她。

monkey
[ˈmʌŋkɪ]

名 猴子

I like the little monkey.
我喜歡那隻小猴子。

the
[ðə]

冠 那個；這個

The Moon rose.
月亮升起。

rain
[ren]

動 下雨

It rains.
下雨了。

小專欄

到目前為止所學的句型，我們來整理一下吧！
1.《主語＋動詞》的句子（沒有補語也沒有受詞）
2.《主語＋動詞＋補語》的句子
3.《主語＋動詞＋受詞》的句子

1.《主語＋動詞》的句子（沒有補語也沒有受詞）

He lives in Taipei.
他住台北。

2.《主語＋動詞＋補語》的句子

Ann became a doctor.
安成為了醫生。

3.《主語＋動詞＋受詞》的句子

I drink milk.
我喝牛奶。

4.有2個受詞的句子（1）

動詞中也有兩的受詞的。這時候的語順是《動詞+間接受詞+直接受詞》。間接受詞一般是「人」，直接受詞一般是「物」。

smile
[smaɪl]

名 微笑
She gave Tom a smile.
她給湯姆一個微笑。

pink
[pɪŋk]

形 粉紅色的
Kate sent me a pink t-shirt.
凱特寄給我一件粉紅色的T恤。

dollar
['dɑlɚ]

名 元

He paid me ninety dollars.
他付了九十元給我。

everything
['ɛvrɪˌθɪŋ]

代 一切

I will tell you everything.
我會告訴你所有的事情。

refrigerator
[rɪ'frɪdʒəˌretɚ]

名 冰箱

Stacy bought her mom a new refrigerator.
史黛西買了一台新冰箱給她母親。

5.有2個受詞的句子（2）

1-39

這類的句型，常用的動詞如下。

everyone (everybody)
['ɛvrɪˌwʌn]

名 每個人

I showed everyone my new car.
我把新車展示給大家看。

grandmother (grandma)
['grændˌmʌðɚ]

名 祖母；奶奶

My grandmother told me a secret.
我的奶奶告訴我一個秘密。

tape
[tep]

名 錄音帶

John sent his girlfriend a tape.
約翰寄了一捲錄音帶給他的女友。

sale
[sel]

名 賣；銷售

He bought me a book from a garage sale.
他在車庫特賣會買了本書給我。

soup
[sup]

名 湯

She made me some pumpkin soup
她為我做些了南瓜湯。

《give+人+物》跟《tell +人+物》的文型，可以把表示人的受詞用 to把受詞的順序前後對調，改成《give+物+to+人》跟《tell +物+to+人》。這時候直接受詞的「物」，變成改寫句的受詞。

《buy+人+物》跟《make+人+物》，可以把表示人的受詞用 for把受詞的順序前後對調，改成寫成《buy+物+for+人》跟《make+物+for+人》。

I told him the truth.
我告訴他真相了。
↓
I told the truth to him.
我告訴他真相了。

He made his mother a cake.
他做了一個生日蛋糕給他媽媽。
↓
He made a cake for his mother.
他做了一個生日蛋糕給他媽媽。

She sent me a card.
她寄給我一張卡片。
↓
She sent a card to me.
她寄給我一張卡片。

He sang me a song.
他唱了一首歌給我聽。
↓
He sang a song for me.
他唱了一首歌給我聽。

6.受詞有補語的句子（1）

1-39

一個句子如果說到受詞，還沒有辦法表達完整的意思，就要在受詞的後面，接跟受詞有對等關係的「受詞補語」。語順是《動詞+受詞+補語》。這類動詞並不多，請把它記住喔！

lead
[lid]

動 帶領
We made him our captain to lead us.
我們選他為隊長來領導我們。

bear
[bɛr]

名 熊；動 忍受
We call the bear Banana.
我們叫這隻熊為香蕉。

baby
['bebɪ]

名 嬰兒
The parents named their baby Pat.
那對父母替嬰兒取名為派特。

ship
[ʃɪp]

名 船
They named the ship Hope.
他們將那條船取名為「希望」。

person
['pɝsn̩]

名 人
I consider him a nice person.
我認為他是一個好人。

7.受詞有補語的句子（2）

1-40

受詞的補語，不僅只有名詞，形容詞也可以當補語。

fan
[fæn]

名 ～迷
The performance made the fans excited.
那場表演讓粉絲們很雀躍。

safe
[sef]

形 安全的
He wants me to be safe and happy.
他希望我平安而且開心。

quite
[kwaɪt]

副 相當
I found the book quite interesting.
我發現這本書相當有趣。

except
[ɪk'sɛpt]

介 除了～之外
He left the windows open except for one.
他把窗子都打開了，只剩一個（關著的）。

traffic
['træfɪk]

名 交通；運輸
The traffic jam drove me crazy.
塞車讓我快瘋了。

1-40

《make+受詞+動詞原形》是「讓…」的使役表現。有這種意思的動詞叫「使役動詞」。

must
[mʌst]

助 必須
I must make her laugh.
我一定要讓她笑。

away
[əˈwe]

副 離開
His mother made him stay away from us
他母親要他離我們遠一點。

perhaps
[pɚˈhæps]

副 或許
Perhaps a walk would make me feel better.
也許走一走會讓我覺得舒服一些。

think
[θɪŋk]

動 認為；思考
What makes you think so?
你怎麼這麼認為呢？

ever
[ˈɛvɚ]

副 曾經
Don't ever make your girlfriend cry.
絕對別讓你女朋友哭。

9.受詞有補語的句子（4）

1-40

Let 也是個使役動詞，《let+受詞+動詞原形》的句型則表示「讓…」、「允許做…」的意思。

least
[list]

形 最小（少）的
Let me at least introduce myself.
至少讓我來自我介紹。

hand
[hænd]

名 手
Let me give you a hand.
我來幫你。

cut
[kʌt]

動 切
Let me cut it in half.
讓我把它切成兩半。

wife
[waɪf]

名 妻子
Please let me see my wife.
請讓我見見我的妻子。

decide
[dɪ'saɪd]

動 決定
Why don't you let her decide?
你為什麼不讓她決定？

10.各種疑問句─what, who等（1）

2-1

　　what表示「什麼」的意思，放在句首，以《what+be動詞+主詞…？》和《what+do+主詞+動詞原形…？》做疑問句。回答的時候不用 yes和no，而是用一般句子。另外，也可用來問事物或職業、身份等。

mean
[min]

動 意指
What does this mean?
這是什麼意思？

lip
[lɪp]

名 嘴唇
What is that on your lips?
你嘴唇上的那是什麼？

September
[sɛp'tɛmbɚ]

名 九月
What are you planning to do in September?
你九月計劃要做什麼？

sixth
[sɪksθ]

形 第六的
What do you want for your sixth anniversary?
結婚六週年慶，你想要什麼？

exciting
[ɪk'saɪtɪŋ]

形 令人興奮的
What exciting things did he say?
那他說了什麼令人興奮的事？

11.各種疑問句─what, who等（2）

who表示「誰」，which表示「哪些，哪一個」，是用來表示疑問的詞，叫「疑問代名詞」。who只用在問人，which表示選擇，用在人或事物都可以。

sweet
[swit]

形 甜的
Who is that sweet girl?
那個甜美的女孩是誰？

she (her,hers, herself)
[ʃi]

代 她（她，她的，她自己）
Who is she?
她是誰？

meal
[mil]

名 餐
Who cooks your meals?
誰料理你的餐食？

white
[hwaɪt]

形 白色的
Which do you like, black or white?
妳喜歡哪一個，黑色或是白色?

right
[raɪt]

名 對的；形 右邊的
Which is the right answer?
哪一個是正確的答案？

12.各種疑問句─what, who等（3）

what和which也用在修飾後面的名詞，表示「什麼的…」、「哪個的…」的用法。

flower
['flauɚ]

名 花
What flowers do you like?
你喜歡什麼花？

p.m.
['pi'ɛm]

代 下午
What time is it now?—It's 9:00p.m..
現在幾點了？－晚上九點了。

size
[saɪz]

名 尺寸

What size is your shirt?
你的襯衫尺寸是幾號的？

towel
[ˈtaʊəl]

名 毛巾

Which towel is mine?
哪一條毛巾是我的？

skirt
[skɝt]

名 裙子

Which skirt suits me the best?
哪一件裙子最適合我？

13.各種疑問句─what, who等（4）

表示「誰的…」用 whose（要記住 who並沒有那個意思喔）。形式是
《whose+名詞》。

whose
[huz]

代 誰的

Whose book is this?
這是誰的書？

belt
[bɛlt]

名 皮帶

Whose belt is this?
這是誰的皮帶？

fire
[faɪr]

名 火

Whose house is on fire?
誰的房子失火了？

jacket
[ˈdʒækɪt]

名 夾克

Whose jacket is gone?
誰的夾克不見了？

ring
[rɪŋ]

動 （鈴）響

Whose mobile is ringing?
誰的手機在響？

14.各種疑問句—when, where等（1）

when用在問時間，表示「什麼時候」；where用在問場所，表示「哪裡」。由於具有副詞的作用，所以又叫做「疑問副詞」。

birthday
[ˈbɝθˌde]
名 生日
When is your birthday?
你的生日是什麼時候？

begin
[bɪˈgɪn]
動 開始
When does the party begin?
舞會幾點開始？

meet
[mit]
動 遇見
When did you meet Lucy?
你什麼時候見過露西？

Friday
[ˈfraɪde]
名 星期五
Where can I go on Friday night?
星期五晚上我可以去哪裡呢？

chair
[tʃɛɚ]
名 椅子
Where did you buy that chair?
你在哪裡買到這張椅子的？

15.各種疑問句—when, where等（2）

why是表示「為什麼」的疑問詞，用在詢問理由、原因。回答 why的疑問句，一般用because來回答。

sure
[ʃʊr]
副 當然
Why are you so sure?
你為何如此篤定？

still
[stɪl]
副 還仍然
Why are you still here?
你為什麼還在這裡？

get [gɛt]	動 得到 Why didn't I get first place? 為什麼我沒有得到第一名？
try [traɪ]	動 試試看 Why don't we try something else? 咱們何不試試別的？
so [so]	副 如此；那麼 Why did you hang out so late? 你為什麼在外面鬼混到這麼晚？

16. 各種疑問句──when, where等（3）

2-3

how是表示「如何」的疑問詞，用在詢問「方法」、「手段」時。

circle ['sɝkl]	名 圈圈 How do you spell the word "circle"? 「圈」這個字（英文）要如何拼呢？
grade [gred]	名 成績 How do you know my grade? 你怎麼知道我的成績？
factory ['fæktərɪ]	名 工廠 How can I get to the factory? 我要怎麼樣去工廠？
finger ['fɪŋgɚ]	名 手指 How did you cut your finger? 你怎麼割到手指的？
that [ðæt]	代 那 How will that help? 那能幫得上什麼忙？

17.各種疑問句─when, where等（4）

how還有詢問健康、天氣「如何」的意思。

partner
['pɑrtnɚ]

名 伙伴，同伙
How are you and your partners?
你和你的夥伴們都好嗎？

eye
[aɪ]

名 眼睛
How is your hurt eye?
你受傷的眼睛還好嗎?

dear
[dɪr]

名 親愛的
How is your dear mother?
你親愛的母親還好嗎？

eve
['iv]

名 前夕
How was your New Year's Eve?
你的除夕夜過的如何？

weather
['wɛðɚ]

名 天氣
How was the weather?
當時的天氣如何？

18.各種疑問句─How old等（1）

How的後面接 old（…歲的）或是 tall（個子高）時，可以用來詢問「幾歲」、「多高」。形式是〈how+形容詞〉。

seventeen
[ˌsɛvən'tin]

名 十七
How old is she? ─She's only seventeen.
她幾歲？─她只有十七歲。

airplane (plane)
['ɛrˌplen]

名 飛機
How old is this airplane?
這架飛機多老了？

waitress
['weɪtrɪs]

名 女服務生
How old is the waitress?
那女服務生幾歲了？

most
[most]

形 大部分的
How tall are most of the players?
大部分的選手有多高？

you (your，yours，yourself，yourselves)
[ju]

代 你（你的，你的，你自己，你們自己）
How tall is your brother?
你弟弟多高？

19. 各種疑問句—How old 等（2）

同樣地，how 的後面接 high（高），long（長），可以用來詢問「高度有多高」、「長度有多長」。

railway
['rel,we]

名 鐵路
How long is that railway?
這條鐵路多長？

trip
[trɪp]

名 旅行
How long was your trip?
你的旅行有多久？

shopkeeper
['ʃɑp,kipɚ]

名 店主
How long will you be the shopkeeper?
你會在這裡當多久的店長？

high
[haɪ]

形 高的
How high is the building?
這棟樓有多高？

mountain
['maʊntn̩]

名 山
How high is that mountain?
那座山有多高？

2-4

How many…是「幾個的…」的意思，how much…是「多少的（量的）…」的意思，可以用來詢問人或事物的數跟量。

socks
[sɑks]

名 短襪
How many socks do you have?
你有多少雙襪子？

dead
[dɛd]

形 死
How many people are dead?
死了多少人？

lesson
[ˈlɛsn̩]

名 課
How many lessons do you have on Monday?
你星期一有幾節課？

cost
[kɔst]

動 花費
How much does this computer cost?
這台電腦多少錢？

candy
[ˈkændɪ]

名 糖果
How much candy did you buy?
你買了多少的糖果？

2-4

How開始的疑問句，常用的有下面的用法。

chicken
[ˈtʃɪkən]

名 雞；雞肉
How much is this chicken?
這隻雞多少錢？

junior high school
[ˈdʒunjɚˌhaɪˌskul]

名 國中
How far is it from here to that junior high school?
從這裡到那間國中有多遠？

face
[fes]

名 臉
How often do you wash your face?
你多久清洗一次臉？

quick
[kwɪk]

形 快的
How quick his reply was!
他的答覆真快！

dangerous
[ˈdendʒərəs]

形 危險的
How dangerous!
多麼危險啊！

22.要注意的疑問句（1）

2-5

疑問詞為主詞的句子，語順跟一般句子一樣是《主詞＋動詞…》。
疑問詞屬第三人稱 單數，所以現在式句中的一般動詞要接-s, -es。

who
[hu]

代 誰
Who plays the piano?
誰會彈鋼琴？

where
[hwɛr]

副 哪裡
Where do your grandparents live?
你的外祖父母住在哪裡？

when
[hwɛn]

副 何時
What do you like to do when you have free time?
妳空閒時喜歡做什麼？

how
[haʊ]

副 如何
How does he get to the train station?
他怎麼去車站的？

why
[hwaɪ]

副 為什麼
Why doesn't Mary come with us?
為什麼瑪莉不和我們一起來？

使用疑問詞 what 來詢問日期、星期、時間也是常用的，要記住喔！

June
[dʒun]

名 六月
What's the date today? —June 6th.
今天幾號？—六月六日。

eight
[et]

名 八
What time is it?—It's eight.
現在幾點？—八點。

Tuesday
['tjuzde]

名 星期二
What day is today?—It's Tuesday.
今天星期幾？—星期二。

what
[hwɑt]

代 什麼
What time is it in New York?
紐約現在幾點？

day
[de]

名 天；日
What day of the week is today?
今天星期幾？

24.要注意的疑問句（3）

2-5

一般的疑問句後面加上《or…》，是表示「…嗎？還是…嗎？」的意思，用來詢問兩個之中的哪一個。回答時不用 yes, no。

cloudy
['klaʊdɪ]

形 多雲的
Is it sunny or cloudy?
天氣是晴朗還是多雲？

sixty
['sɪkstɪ]

名 六十
Is David 59 or 60 (sixty)years old?—He's 59 years old.
大衛59歲還是60歲？—他59歲。

yellow
['jɛlo]

名 黃色的
Is this yellow or blue?—It's blue.
這是黃色還是藍色?—是藍色。

leave
[liv]

動 遺留; 離開
Is he leaving or entering?—He's leaving.
他要進來還是出去?—他要出去。

taxi
['tæksɪ]

名 計程車
Do you walk or take a taxi?—I walk.
你是走路還是搭計程車?—我走路。

25.要注意的疑問句(4)

2-6

以 which(哪個,哪邊)為句首的疑問句,後面也有接《A or B》(A還是B)的形式。

Coke
[kok]

名 可樂
Which do you want, beer or Coke?
你想要哪一個,啤酒還是可樂?

ham
[hæm]

名 火腿
Which do you like, ham or sausage?
妳比較喜歡火腿還是香腸?

which
[hwɪtʃ]

形 哪一個
Which is Ann's, this or that?
哪一個是安的,這個還是那個?

telephone (phone)
['tɛlə,fon]

名 電話
Which does he prefer, e-mail or telephone?
他比較喜歡電子郵件還是電話?

season
['sizn̩]

名 季節
Which season do you like, spring or summer?
你比較喜歡哪個季節?春天還是夏天?

26.各種否定句（1）

不用 not也能表示否定的意思。如把副詞 never放在動詞的前面，就有「絕對沒有…」，表示強烈否定的意味。

holiday
['hɑlə,de]
名 假期
I'll never forget that special holiday
我永遠不會忘記那次特別的假日。

trouble
['trʌbl]
名 麻煩
She never gets herself in trouble.
她從沒讓自己惹過麻煩。

fork
[fɔrk]
名 叉子
Never bite your fork like that again.
絕對不准再像那樣咬你的叉子。

never
['nɛvɚ]
副 從不
Never give up.
絕對不要放棄！

should
[ʃʊd]
助 應該
You should never break your promise.
你永遠都不該違背你的承諾。

27.各種否定句（2）

not跟 very（非常）、always（總是）、all（全部的）、every（每一的）等字一起使用，就有「不是全部…」的意思，也就是部份否定。

story
['storɪ]
名 故事
I don't like the story very much.
我不怎麼喜歡這個故事。

band
[bænd]
名 樂團
Patty didn't like the band very much.
派蒂以前不怎麼喜歡那個樂團。

always
['ɔlwez]

副 總是

Iris is not always right.
艾瑞絲並非總是對的。

happy
['hæpɪ]

形 快樂的；幸福的

He doesn't feel happy all the time.
他並不是所有時候都很快樂。

art
[ɑrt]

名 藝術

Not every man can understand art.
不是所有的人都能瞭解藝術。

28.各種否定句（3）

2-7

用形容詞的 no也可以表示否定。用《no+名詞》就有「一點…也沒有」、「一個…也沒有」的意思。No的後面，單複數都可以接。

color
['kʌlɚ]

名 顏色

The dog sees no color.
狗看不見顏色。

farmer
['farmɚ]

名 農夫

The farmer has no children.
那位農夫沒有小孩。

nose
[noz]

名 鼻子

This doll has no nose.
這洋娃娃沒有鼻子。

March
[mɑrtʃ]

名 三月

There are no holidays in March.
三月沒有假日。

real
['rɪəl]

形 真的

The old saying "no pain, no gain" is real.
那句古老諺語「一分耕耘，一分收穫」是真的。

29.各種否定句（4）

用 nothing（無一物）、nobody（無一人）或 no one（無一人）也可以表示否定的意思。

nothing
[ˈnʌθɪŋ]

代 沒什麼
I have nothing to do today.
我今天沒事做。

popular
[ˈpɑpjələ]

形 受歡迎的；流行的
She knows nothing about popular music.
她對流行音樂一無所知。

path
[pæθ]

名 小路，小徑
Nobody took that path.
沒人走過那條路。

nobody
[ˈnoˌbɑdɪ]

形 沒有人
Nobody likes losing.
沒有人喜歡失敗。

strong
[strɔŋ]

形 強壯的
No one is strong enough to move that box.
沒有人強壯到足以移動那個箱子。

30.命令句（1）

命令對方的句子叫做命令句。命令句不用主詞，用動詞原形開始。

off
[ɔf]

副 扣除
Take off your hat!
把你的帽子脫掉！

gas
[gæs]

名 瓦斯；汽油
Turn off the gas!
把瓦斯關掉！

108

sofa [ˈsofə]	名 沙發 Move that sofa away. 把那沙發移開。
sidewalk [ˈsaɪdˌwɔlk]	名 行人穿越道 Stay on the sidewalk, please. 請待在人行道上。
Earth [ɝθ]	名 地球 Please protect our Earth. 請保護我們的地球。

31.命令句（2）

2-8

表示「別做⋯」的否定命令文，要把 don't 放在句首，形式是《don't+動詞原形⋯》。

care [kɛr]	動 擔心 Don't care too much. 別太在意。
cheese [tʃiz]	名 乳酪 Don't eat the cheese. 別吃這乳酪。
May [me]	名 五月 Don't forget our trip in May! 別忘了我們五月的旅行!
green [grin]	名 綠色的 Please don't pick the green one. 拜託別選綠色的那個。
snack [snæk]	名 零食 Please don't eat snacks before dinner. 請不要在晚餐前吃零食。

32.命令句（3）

2-8

用《Let's+動詞原形…》（讓…吧）形式，是提議對方做某事的說法。若回答好用「Yes, let's」，不好則用「No, let's not.」。

picnic
['pɪknɪk]

名 野餐
Let's go on a picnic!
去野餐吧！

north
[nɔrθ]

名 北方
Let's travel north.
我們往北方旅行吧！

rainbow
['ren,bo]

名 彩虹
Let's take a photo of that rainbow!
我們來給那彩虹拍張照吧！

jog
['dʒɑg]

動 慢跑
Let's go jogging in the park.
我們到公園慢跑吧！

zoo
[zu]

名 動物園
Let's go to the zoo, kids.
孩子們，我們去動物園吧！

33.命令句（4）

2-8

命令句是用動詞原形為句首，所以 be動詞的命令句就是用 Be來開頭，表示「要…」的意思。否定的命令句，也是在 be動詞的前面接Don't。

ready
['rɛdɪ]

形 準備好了
Be ready for the test.
準備好要考試。

arm
[ɑrm]

名 手臂
Be careful with your arm.
小心你的手臂。

110

animal
['ænəml]
名 動物
Be kind to animals.
要善待動物。

excited
[ɪk'saɪtɪd]
形 感到興奮的
Don't get too excited.
別太興奮。

anyone (anybody)
['ɛnɪˌwʌn]
代 任何人（任何人）
Don't trust anyone.
別相信任何人。

34.感歎句（1）

2-9

用《What (+a〔an〕)+形容詞+名詞》開始的句子，然後再接《主詞＋動詞！》，就是表示強烈的情緒或感情的句子，意思是「真是…啊！」。

space
[spes]
名 太空；空間
What a huge space!
好大的空間喔！

restroom
['rɛstˌrum]
名 洗手間
What a dirty restroom!
好髒的廁所喔！

mouth
[maʊθ]
名 嘴
What a big mouth she has!
她的嘴巴好大喔！

cheap
[tʃip]
名 便宜
What cheap clothes they are!
好便宜的衣服喔！

windy
['wɪndɪ]
形 多風的
What a windy day it is!
（天氣）風好大啊！

35.感嘆句（2）

這種表示強烈感情的句子叫「感嘆句」。感嘆文句尾要用驚嘆號「！」。感嘆句常省略主詞和動詞。

animal
['ænəml]

名 動物
What a funny animal(it is)!
多麼有趣的動物啊！

useful
['jusfəl]

形 有用的
What a useful tool(it is)!
真好用的工具！

garden
['ɡɑrdn̩]

名 花園
What a large garden(it is)!
好大的花園喔！

surprise
[sə'praɪz]

動 使～吃驚；名 驚奇的事
What a surprise(it is)!
多麼驚奇啊！

sunny
['sʌnɪ]

形 晴朗的
What a sunny day(it is)!
多晴朗的一天啊！

36.感嘆句（3）

用《How+形容詞+主詞+動詞！》表示「多麼…啊！」的意思。這時候 how 的後面不接 a。

lucky
['lʌkɪ]

形 幸運的
How lucky he is!
他真幸運啊！

shy
[ʃaɪ]

形 害羞的
How shy you are!
你真害羞耶！

polite
[pə'laɪt]

形 有禮貌的；客氣的
How polite he is!
他好有禮貌喔！

difficult
['dɪfəkʌlt]

形 困難的
How difficult this task is!
這任務真困難！

wonderful
['wʌndɚfəl]

形 奇妙的
How wonderful it is!
這真是太好了！

37.感嘆句（4）

2-9

How的感嘆句，有時後面不是接形容詞，而是接副詞。用《How+副詞+主詞+動詞》，表示「多麼…啊！」。

patient
['peʃənt]

形 有耐心的
How slowly that patient man does his work!
那位有耐心的男士做事還真慢啊！

strange
[strendʒ]

形 奇怪的
How strangely he behaves! What a strange person!
他的行為好怪！真是個怪咖！

dress
[drɛs]

名 洋裝；動 穿
How perfectly she dresses!
她穿得真好！

light
[laɪt]

形 輕的 ；名 燈
How late the light invented was!
燈發明得真晚啊！

perfect
['pɝfɪkt]

形 完美的
How quickly you found your perfect match!
你真快就找到你的完美拍檔了！

1.比較級的用法（1）

表示比較的形容詞叫「比較級」。用《比較級形容詞+than…》來比較兩者之間，意思是「…比…為…」。比較級一般是在形容詞的詞尾加 -er。比較的對象用 than…表示。

warm
[wɔrm]

形 溫暖的
It is warmer inside than outside.
裡面比外面溫暖。

a lot
[ə lɑt]

副 許多
Jack is a lot smarter than Pat.
傑克比派特聰明得多。

almost
['ɔl,most]

副 幾乎
The cat is almost bigger than the dog.
這隻貓幾乎比那隻狗還大。

both
[boθ]

代 兩者皆是
She is younger than both of you.
她比你們兩個都年輕。

math
[mæθ]

名 數學
The English test is easier than the math test.
英文試題比數學簡單。

2.比較級的用法（2）

副詞也可以和形容詞一樣形成比較級。用《副詞的比較級+than…》表示「比…還…」的意思。副詞比較級的作法跟形容詞一樣。

train
[tren]

名 火車
The train runs faster than my car.
那輛火車跑得比我的車子快。

a little
[ə'lɪtl]

片 一點
I can walk a little further than you.
我可以比你走更遠一些。

114

seldom
['sɛldəm]

副 很少
Rob seldom studies harder than Nelson.
羅伯很少會比尼爾森努力學習。

burn
[bɜn]

動 燃燒
Wood can burn longer than paper.
木頭比紙張要能燒得更久。

slow
[slo]

形 慢的
You can't drive slower than I.
你不可能比我還開得更慢了。

3.比較級的用法（3）

2-10

形容詞或副詞比較長的時候，前面接 more就形成比較級了。形式是《more+形容詞或副詞+than…》。

health
[hɛlθ]

名 健康
Health is more important than wealth.
健康比財富更重要。

more
[mor]

形 更多的
Laura is more beautiful than Patty.
萊拉比派蒂更美。

pull
[pʊl]

動 拉
He pulled harder than I.
他拉得比我還要用力。

people
['pipḷ]

名 人們
Bill has more confidence than any other people.
比爾比任何人都有自信。

air
[ɛr]

名 空氣
Air in the forest is fresher than that in the city.
森林裡的空氣比城市裡的要新鮮。

比較句中也可以省略 than…的部分。這是用在不必說出 than…，也能知道比較的對象時。

pants
[pænts]

名 褲子

His pants are longer.
他的褲子比較長。

pork
[pork]

名 豬肉

I like pork better.
我比較喜歡豬肉。

voice
[vɔɪs]

名 聲音

Her voice is louder.
她的聲音比較大。

shall
[ʃæl]

助 將

I shall run faster.
我要跑快一點。

possible
[ˈpɑsəbl̩]

形 可能的

Please speak more slowly if possible.
可能的話，請講更慢一點。

5.最高級的形成（1）

三者以上的比較，表示「最…的」的形容詞叫「最高級形容詞」。而在其前面加定冠詞 the，成為《the+最高級形容詞》的形式。最高級一般在形容詞詞尾加 -est。

bright
[braɪt]

形 明亮的

This star is the brightest of the four.
那顆星星是四顆中最亮的。

queen
[kwin]

名 王后

She is the youngest queen ever.
她是有史以來最年輕的皇后。

photographer
[fə'tɑgrəfɚ]

名 攝影師
He is the best photographer in the competition.
他是比賽中最好的攝影師。

bakery
['bekərɪ]

名 麵包店
This is the best bread in the bakery.
這是麵包店裡最棒的麵包。

spoon
[spun]

名 湯匙
That is the biggest spoon I've got.
那是我所有的最大的湯匙了。

6.最高級的形成（2）

2-11

副詞也可以和形容詞一樣，形成最高級副詞。用《the+最高級副詞》表示三者以上之間的比較「最…」的意思，用法跟形容詞一樣。這時候，the常有被省略的情況。

group
[grup]

名 群體
Mike runs the fastest in group three
麥克是第三組中跑得最快的。

fisherman
['fɪʃəmən]

名 漁夫
That fisherman can dive the deepest in the ocean.
在海裡，那個漁夫能潛到最深。

West
[wɛst]

名 西方
Oliver is the best scientist in the West
歐立弗是西方最優秀的科學家。

loud
[laʊd]

形 大聲的
Kate sang the loudest in the chorus.
凱特是合唱團裡唱最大聲的。

age
[edʒ]

名 年齡
Mary thinks the deepest of the girls her age.
瑪莉在同年齡的女孩中想最深入。

7.最高級的形成（3）

形容詞或副詞比較長的時候，前面接 most就形成最高級了。形式是《the most+形容詞或副詞》。

hat
[hæt]

名 帽子（有邊的）
This hat is the most expensive of the three.
這頂帽子是三頂中最貴的。

PE
['pi'i]

名 體育課
PE is the most interesting subject to me.
體育課對我來說是最有趣的科目。

expensive
[ɪk͵spɛnsɪv]

形 昂貴的
The bag is the most expensive one in the store.
那包包是全店最貴的一個。

world
[wɜld]

名 世界
Christ is the most famous rock star in the world.
克斯特是全世界最有名的搖滾明星。

tomato
[tə'meto]

名 蕃茄
Tomatoes are the most disgusting food in the world!
蕃茄是世界上最噁心的食物！

8.最高級的形成（4）

最高級形容詞也可以用來修飾複數名詞，用《one of the+最高級形容詞+名詞》表示「最好的…之一」。這是最高級常用的說法。

language
['læŋgwɪdʒ]

名 語言
Chinese is one of the most difficult languages.
中文是最困難的語言之一。

writer
['raɪtɚ]

名 作家
She is one of the richest writers in the world.
她是全世界最有錢的作家之一。

festival
['fɛstəvl]

名 節日
This is one of the most important festivals.
這是最重要的節日之一。

lion
['laɪən]

名 獅子
The lion is the strongest animal in the forest.
獅子是森林裡最強壯的動物。

important
[ɪm'pɔrtn̩t]

形 重要的
Rita is one of the most important players in this game.
麗塔是這場比賽中最重要的選手之一。

9.副詞的比較級

2-12

想要做誰「跑得比較快」、「跳得比較遠」這種動作的比較時，會用到副詞的比較級。副詞的比較級和一般的比較級差不多，同樣也是《形容詞＋er》，只是放置的位置在動詞後，用來修飾動詞。

type
[taɪp]

動 打字
She types faster than he.
她打字打得比他快。

human
['hjumən]

形 人類的；名 人類
Humans think more than other animals.
人類想得比其他動物要多。

hip
[hɪp]

名 屁股，臀部
Patty has hips wider than mine.
派蒂的臀部比我的寬。

powerful
['pauɚfəl]

形 強大的，作用大的
Sam is more powerful than you.
山姆比你還有力量。

vendor
['vɛndɚ]

名 小販，攤販
The street vendor earns more than you.
那個小販賺的比你多。

人們聚在一起常會比較個高下，要選出最好的，會用副詞的最高級。它和一般的最高級相同，同樣也是《形容詞＋est》或《the most ＋形容詞》；只是位置是在動詞後，用來修飾動詞。

stage [stedʒ]	名 舞台 He does the greatest performance on stage. 他在舞台上做最棒的演出。
income [ˈɪnˌkʌm]	名 收入 Jenny has the highest income in her office. 珍妮是全辦公室裡收入最高的。
spaghetti [spəˈgɛtɪ]	名 義大利麵 I make the best spaghetti in my family. 我是我家裡做義大利麵做得最好吃的。
violin [ˌvaɪəˈlɪn]	名 小提琴 Rita bought the most expensive violin in that shop. 麗塔買了那家店裡最昂貴的小提琴。
winner [ˈwɪnɚ]	名 獲勝者 The winner did the best of all the competitors. 優勝者是參賽者裡最好的一位。

11.副詞比較級—like…better

2-13

在遇到二選一的狀況時，可以用《like…better than…》從中挑出自己比較喜愛、偏好的一項。要注意喔！like和than後面接的選項要對稱，例如：前面是名詞，後面也要是名詞。

action [ˈækʃən]	名 行動，活動 Jill likes action movies better than comedies. 吉兒喜歡動作片勝過喜劇片。
guitar [gɪˈtɑr]	名 吉他 I like guitar better than violin. 我喜歡吉他勝過小提琴。

natural
['nætʃərəl]

形 自然的，天然的

They like natural juice better than coffee.

她們喜歡天然果汁勝過咖啡。

guava
['gwɑvə]

名 芭樂，番石榴

Kim likes oranges better than guavas.

金喜歡柳丁勝過番石榴。

model
['mɑdl̩]

名 模範，模特兒;; 動 塑造

We like this model better than the other one.

我們喜歡這個模特兒勝過另一個（模特兒）。

12.副詞最高級—like…the best

用英文介紹自己的最愛，要這麼說：《人＋like/ love＋最喜歡的事物＋the best》，當人是《第三人稱‧單數》時，要把like或love加上s喔。

bean
[bin]

名 豆類，豆莢

Jack likes red bean soup the best.

傑克最喜歡紅豆湯。

bowling
['bolɪŋ]

名 保齡球，投球

We love bowling the best.

我們最喜歡保齡球。

cartoon
[kɑr'tun]

名 卡通，連環漫畫

He loves cartoons the best.

他最喜歡卡通。

culture
['kʌltʃɚ]

名 文化

They like Chinese culture the best.

他們最喜歡中國文化。

crayon
['kreən]

名 蠟筆，炭筆

Mandy likes crayons the best.

曼蒂最喜歡蠟筆。

當面臨兩個選擇都不錯，又不想得罪任何一方，就說兩者都「一樣棒」、「一樣好」，是並駕齊驅的狀態，這時用《人＋be動詞＋as＋比較項目＋as＋比較對象》可以婉轉地表達。

ant
[ænt]

名 螞蟻

He is as hard-working as an ant.
他像螞蟻一樣努力。

adult
[ə'dʌlt]

名 成年人; 形 成年的

Zack is as tall as an adult
查克和一個成年人一樣高。

angel
['endʒl]

名 天使，守護神

Linda is as beautiful as an angel.
琳達和天使一樣美。

confident
['kɑnfədənt]

形 確信的，有信心的，自信的

Kate is as confident as David.
凱特和大衛一樣有自信。

Confucius
[kən'fjuʃəs]

名 孔子

She is as smart as Confucius.
她和孔子一樣聰明。

1.現在完成式的用法─完了‧結果（1）
2-14

「現在完成式」是用來表示，到現在為止跟現在有關的動作或狀態。用《have+過去分詞》的形式。現在完成式含有「過去＋現在」的語意。常跟just（剛剛）連用，表示剛做完的動作，意思是「（現在）剛…」。

just
[dʒʌst]

副 只是；剛剛才

I have just finished my work.
我才剛完成我的工作。

store
[stor]

名 商店

I have just left that store.
我才剛離開那家店。

ice cream
['aɪsˌkrim']

名 冰淇淋
She has just finished her icecream.
她剛吃完她的冰淇淋。

church
[tʃɝtʃ]

名 教堂
Mary has just gone to the church.
瑪莉剛剛才去教堂。

floor
[flor]

名 地板
Have you just mopped the floor?
你剛拖了地板嗎?

2.現在完成式的用法—完了‧結果（2）

2-14

現在完成式還表示動作結束了，而其結果現在還留的狀態。意思是「（已經）…了」。

lose
[luz]

動 輸；失去
I have lost my pen.
我丟了筆。

cold
[kold]

形 冷的；名 感冒
I have got a cold.
我著涼了。

job
[dʒɑb]

名 工作
I have got a new job.
我找到一份新工作。

word
[wɝd]

名 字；單字
My mother has taught me a new word.
我媽媽教了我一個新單字。

million
['mɪljən]

名 百萬
He has saved a million dollars
他已經存了一百萬元。

2-14

表示動作「完了」、「結果」用法的否定句，常用副詞 yet，表示動作還沒有完成，意思是「還沒…」。

yet
[jɛt]

副 尚未；還沒
I have not seen the movie yet.
我還沒去看那部電影。

waiter
['wetɚ]

名 服務生
The waiter has not come yet.
服務生還沒來。

Mr.
['mɪstɚ]

名 先生
I have not spoken to Mr. Lin yet.
我尚未和林先生說話。

workbook
['wɝk,bʊk]

名 習作簿
I have not found my workbook yet.
我還沒找到我的習作簿。

way
[we]

名 方法；路
I haven't found the way to the gym yet.
我還沒找到去體育館的路。

2-15

動作「完了、結果」用法的疑問句，常用副詞 yet，來詢問動作完成了沒有。意思是「（已經）做了…沒？」。

part
[pɑrt]

名 部分
Have you finished your part yet?
你完成你的那部份了嗎？

stop
[stɑp]

動 停
Has it stopped raining yet?
雨停了沒有？

police [pə'lis]	名 警察 Has he called the police yet? 他打電話給警察了沒有？
worker ['wɝkɚ]	名 工人 Have the workers finished yet? 工人做完了沒有？
fix [fɪks]	動 修理 Have they fixed the computer yet? 他們修理電腦了沒？

5.現在完成式的用法─繼續（1）

2-15

現在完成式，用來表示從過去繼續到現在的動作或狀態。意思是「（現在仍然）…著」。這時候常跟表示過去已結束的某一期間的 for（…之久），或表示從過去某時起，直到說話現在時的 since（自…以來）連用。

ROC ['ɑr'o'si]	名 中華民國 She has lived in Taiwan, the R.O.C, for six years. 她住在中華民國已經六年了。
case [kes]	名 事件 We have worked on this case for many years. 我們處理這件案子已經很多年了。
date [det]	名 日期；動 約會 We have dated for three years. 我們交往已經有三年了。
worry ['wɝɪ]	動 擔心 I have been worried about you since then. 我從那時以來就一直很擔心你。
repeat [rɪ'pit]	動 重複 She has repeated the same thing for ten minutes. 她已經重複同樣的東西有十分鐘了。

表示「繼續」的用法時，be動詞也可以成為現在完成式。be動詞的過去分詞是 been。

since
[sɪns]

連 從～以來
I've been busy since yesterday.
從昨天開始我就很忙了。

beside
[bɪ'saɪd]

介 在～之間
I've been standing beside you for ten minutes.
我站在妳旁邊十分鐘了。

pizza
['pɪzə]

名 披薩
I've been making pizza since noon.
我從中午就一直在做披薩。

then
[ðen]

副 那麼；當時；然後
What's he been doing since then?
從那時到現在，他都在幹什麼？

knock
[nɑk]

動 敲
Why have you been knocking at the door?
你剛剛為何一直在敲門？

現在完成式的疑問句可以用 How long開頭，來詢問繼續的「期間」。這時候要用 For…或 Since…來回答。

history
['hɪstrɪ]

名 歷史
How long have you been studying history?
你讀歷史讀多久了？

cheat
[tʃit]

動 欺騙
How long have you been cheating on me?
你欺騙了我多久了？

126

build [bɪld]	動 建造 How long have you been building this house? 你這房子蓋多久了？
ten [tɛn]	名 十 —For ten years. 已經十年了。
February [ˈfɛbruˌɛrɪ]	名 二月 —Since February, 1987. 從1987年二月開始就住這裡了。

8.現在完成式的用法─繼續（4）

「繼續」用法的否定句，表示「（現在仍然）沒有…」的意思。

October [ɑkˈtobɚ]	名 十月 I haven't seen him since last October. 我從去年十月起就沒看到他了。
medicine [ˈmɛdəsn̩]	名 藥 You haven't taken the medicine yet? 你還沒吃藥？
place [ples]	名 地方 I haven't been to this place before. 我以前沒來過這個地方。
island [ˈaɪlənd]	名 島嶼 They haven't found the island yet. 他們還沒找到那座島。
over [ˈovɚ]	介 結束的 We haven't finished the movie yet. It's not over. 我們還沒看完電影，它還沒結束。

9.現在完成式的用法──經驗（1）

2-16

表示從過去直到現在為止的經驗，意思是「（到現在為止）曾經…」。這時候常跟twice（兩次）, once（一次）, before（從前）, often（時常）, …times（次）等副詞連用。

miss
[mɪs]

動 錯過
I've missed the show twice.
我已經錯過這節目兩次了。

once
[wʌns]

副 一次
I've been there once.
我曾經去過那裡一次。

lake
[lek]

名 湖
He has been to that lake before.
他之前就去過那座湖了。

to
[tu]

介 向；對
John has gone to Japan often.
約翰常去日本。

habit
['hæbɪt]

名 習慣
Jane has tried giving up that bad habit many times.
珍試著戒除那壞習慣很多次了。

10.現在完成式的用法──經驗（2）

2-17

「經驗」用法的否定句，常用 never（從未…，從不…）。

say
[se]

動 說
I have never said that.
我從來沒有說過（那些話）。

China
['tʃaɪnə]

名 中國
I have never been to China.
我從來沒有去過中國。

128

bicycle (bike)
['baɪsɪk!]

名 腳踏車
He has never ridden a bike.
他從來沒有騎過腳踏車。

star
[star]

名 星星，明星；動 由～主演
I've never met any movie stars before.
我以前從來沒有遇見過電影明星。

thing
[θɪŋ]

名 事情
Laura has never forgotten a thing.
蘿拉從來沒有忘記任何事情。

11 現在完成式的用法—經驗（3）

2-17

詢問「經驗」的現在完成式疑問句，常用副詞 ever（曾經）。ever要放在過去分詞的前面。

hear
[hɪr]

動 聽
Have you ever heard him sing?
你聽過他唱歌嗎？

visit
['vɪzɪt]

動 拜訪
Have you ever visited Nara?
你參觀過奈良嗎？

practice
['præktɪs]

動 練習
Have you ever practiced English with an American?
你曾經和美國人練習英文過嗎？

snow
[sno]

動 下雪；名 雪
Have you ever seen snow?
你看過雪嗎？

game
[gem]

名 遊戲
Has he ever played this game?
他玩過這遊戲嗎？

2-17

可以用 How many times或 How often做開頭，成為現在完成式的疑問句，來詢問「曾經做過幾次」。

lend
[lɛnd]

動 借出
How many times have you lent him money?
你借過他幾次錢了？

homework
['hom,wɜk]

名 功課；作業
How many times have I told you? Do your homework!
我跟你說過幾次了？做你的作業！

along
[ə'lɔŋ]

介 沿著；副 一起
How many times has he come along with you?
他和你一起來幾次了？

clean
[klin]

動 清掃
How often has he cleaned his room?
他多常清理他的房間？

bottom
['bɑtəm]

名 底部
How often have we washed the bottom of the sink?
我們多常清洗水槽的底部？

1.介系詞的功能及意思（1）

2-18

介系詞是放在名詞或名詞相當詞之前，來表示該名詞等和句中其他詞之間的關係的詞。at用在表示時間上的一點，如時刻等；in表示較長的時間，用在上下午、週、月、季節及年等；on用在日或某日上下午等。

born
[bɔrn]

動 出生
He was born in 1865.
他是1865年生的。

a.m.
[e][ɛm]

片 上午
We can meet in the morning. How about 9:00 a.m.?
我們可以下午見面。九點如何?

winter
['wɪntɚ]

名 冬天
It is hard to find wild animals in winter.
冬天很難找到野生動物。

program
['progræm]

名 節目
The TV program begins at eight o'clock.
這電視節目八點開始。

April
['eprəl]

名 四月
We play jokes on our friends on April 1st..
我們四月一號都會開朋友玩笑。

2.介系詞的功能及意思（2）

2-18

下面這些片語，要記住喔！

machine
[mə'ʃin]

名 機械
Ann turns on the machine in the morning.
安在早上把機器打開。

November
[no'vɛmbɚ]

名 十一月
Patty came here in November.
派蒂十一月到這裡的。

oil
[ɔɪl]

名 油
Don't burn the midnight oil too often.
別太常熬夜。

living room
['lɪvɪŋ,rum]

名 客廳
He cleans the living room on Sunday morning.
他星期天早上打掃客廳。

square
[skwɛr]

名 廣場
I want to go to the square on Friday.
星期五我想去廣場。

3.介系詞的功能及意思（3）

區分下列這些介系詞的不同：表示動作完成的期限 by（最遲在…以前），表示動作繼續的終點 until（直到）；表示期間 for，表示某狀態繼續的期間 during。

fifth
['fɪfθ]

形 第五的
I'll finish my plan by the fifth of July.
我會在七月五號以前完成我的計畫。

until
[ən'tɪl]

介 直到
We watched TV until ten o'clock.
我們看電視看到十點。

into
['ɪntə]

介 到～之內
She went deep into the forest and stayed for a month.
她深入森林裡並且停留了一個月。

low
[lo]

形 低
She spoke in a low voice during the speech.
在演講時她很小聲說話。

noon
[nun]

名 中午
We played basketball till noon.
我們打籃球打到中午。

4.介系詞的功能及意思（4）

用在一地點或比較小的地方 at（在），用在較大的地方 in（在）；緊貼在上面 on（在上面），中間有距離的在上面 above（在上）。under（在下面）在正下方。

turn
[tɝn]

動 轉
The truck turned right at the corner.
卡車在轉角處右轉。

dig
[dɪg]

動 挖
They are digging a hole in the backyard.
他們正在後院挖洞。

pie
[paɪ]

名 派
Your apple pie is on the table.
你的蘋果派在桌上。

above
[ə'bʌv]

介 在～之上
Our plane is flying above the clouds.
我們的飛機正飛翔在雲端。

under
['ʌndə]

介 在～底下
The cat is under the desk.
貓在書桌底下。

5.介系詞的功能及意思（5）

2-19

各種介系詞的位置關係。

bedroom
['bɛd,rum]

名 臥室
He is in the bedroom.
他在臥房裡。

desk
[dɛsk]

名 書桌
My notes are on my desk.
我的筆記在書桌上。

beside
[bɪ'saɪd]

介 在～旁邊
The ball is beside the box.
球在箱子旁邊。

put
[pʊt]

動 放
I put the ball under the box.
我把球放在箱子下。

behind
[bɪ'haɪnd]

介 在～之後
The ball is behind the box.
球在箱子後面。

6.By以外的介系詞

除了可以用by來說明是誰做的動作，不同的介係詞和動詞組成慣用的片語，還有其他不同的意思，像是：「be interested in+有興趣的對象」、「be excited about+感到興奮的對象」、「be surprised at+感到驚訝的事物」…。

interested
['ɪntrɪstɪd]
形 感到有趣的
My brother is interested in music.
我弟弟對音樂很有興趣。

business
['bɪznɪs]
名 商業
We are all excited about this big business.
我們都對這筆大生意感到興奮。

fact
[fækt]
名 事實
I am surprised at the scientific fact.
我對那個科學證實感到驚訝。

thirteen
[θɝ'tin]
名 十三
All tickets were sold out in thirteen minutes
所有票都在十三分鐘內賣完。

bowl
[bol]
名 碗
This bowl is made of glass.
這個碗是用玻璃做的。

1.用by來表示動作者

被動式就是「被…」的意思，主要的結構是《主詞＋be動詞＋過去分詞》，若是想要特別說明是「被誰…」，那就要主要結構後面加上《by+動作者》。

cow
[kaʊ]
名 母牛
The grass is eaten by the cow.
草被母牛吃掉了。

glove
[glʌv]
名 手套
Those new gloves are made by the designer.
這些新手套是那位設計師做的。

hit [hɪt]	動 打 John is hit by a ball. 約翰被球打到。
by [baɪ]	介 被 Mr. Brown is loved by his students. 伯朗先生受學生喜愛。
very [ˈvɛrɪ]	副 非常；很 I'm very sure that this e-mail was not written by her. 我很確定這封電子郵件不是她寫的。

2.行為者不明

2-20

被動式中，不清楚是誰做的動作時，可以不用加上「被誰…」來說明做動作的人。只要講出《主詞＋be動詞＋過去分詞》來說明「接收動作的人，接受到怎樣的動作」就可以了。

down [daʊn]	副 向下；由上而下 What he said was written down. 他說的話被寫下來了。
ago [əˈgo]	副 在～以前 The church was built many years ago. 這座教堂是好幾年前建造的。
public [ˈpʌblɪk]	形 公共的 My wallet was stolen in a public restroom. 我的錢包在公共廁所被偷了。
many [ˈmɛnɪ]	形 許多的 Many of us were invited to Lisa's party. 我們之中很多人受邀參加麗沙的派對。
different [ˈdɪfərənt]	形 不同的 This novel is written in different languages. 這本小說是用不同語言寫的。

被動式的疑問句,是把直述句主要結構中的be動詞移到句首,變成《be動詞+主詞+過去分詞?》這樣的問句結構。

take
[tek]

動 搭乘;帶
Is this seat taken?
這個位子有人坐嗎?

thousand
['θauzənd]

名 千
Is it the year two-thousand-eight?
是西元兩千零八年嗎?

kill
[kɪl]

動 殺
Was the man killed?
那男人被殺了嗎?

finish
['fɪnɪʃ]

動 舉行
Is this meeting finished?
這場會議結束了嗎?

land
[lænd]

名 土地
Is the land sold?
那塊土地被賣掉了嗎?

1.名詞的用法

2-21

不定詞主要的功能是讓一個句子裡,不會同時出現兩個動詞,而造成錯誤文法。舉例來說:want (to go) 的用法,可避免want和go兩個動詞同時存在,這時,不定詞具有名詞的性質。

cross
[krɔs]

動 越過;穿過
I want to cross the street.
我想過馬路。

count
[kaunt]

動 計算
They started to count from one to a hundred.
他們開始從一數到一百。

fifteen
[fɪfˈtin]

名 十五
I would like to leave within fifteen minutes.
我想要再十五分鐘以內離開。

hospital
[ˈhɑspɪt!]

名 醫院
My father wanted to leave the hospital.
我爸爸想要離開醫院。

body
[ˈbɑdɪ]

名 身體
I need to keep my body in shape.
我需要保持我的身材。

2.副詞的用法（1）

2-21

不定詞也可以當作副詞來使用，舉例來說：I use this notebook.（我用這本筆記本）已經是句完整的句子，若想要詳細說明筆記本的用途，就加上to keep a diary（寫日記），當作副詞來修飾use的用途（目的）。

knee
[ni]

名 膝蓋
I use this to protect my knees.
我用這個來保護我的膝蓋。

snake
[snek]

名 蛇
My father asked me to stay away from the snake.
我爸爸叫我離那條蛇遠一點。

bite
[baɪt]

動 咬
His dog bites the toys to sharpen its teeth.
他的狗啃咬玩具來磨牙。

borrow
[ˈbɑro]

動 借入
The Lins borrowed some money to buy a house.
林家人借了一些錢來買房子。

heat
[hit]

動 加熱；名 熱度
I turned on the stove to heat up the soup.
我把爐子打開，把湯加熱。

3.副詞的用法（2）

不定詞當副詞使用時，除了修飾動詞、也可以修飾形容詞，主要的結構是《主詞＋be動詞＋形容詞＋不定詞》，其中的不定詞用來修飾形容詞，表示其原因。

typhoon
[taɪˈfun]

名 颱風
I am glad to have a sunny day after a horrible typhoon.
我很高興在可怕的颱風後看到一個晴朗的天氣。

matter
[ˈmætɚ]

名 事情；情況
I am sorry to hear about the matter.
聽說了這件事情我感到遺憾。

stomach
[ˈstʌmək]

名 胃
He is nervous about seeing the medical report about his stomach.
他因為要看自己的胃部醫療報告而感到緊張。

dozen
[ˈdʌzn̩]

名 一打
Judy is happy to receive a dozen roses.
茱蒂收到一打的玫瑰花很開心。

proud
[praʊd]

形 驕傲的；得意的
Larry is proud to win the prize.
賴瑞很得意能得獎。

4.形容詞的用法

不定詞也可以當作形容詞來使用，位置是接在名詞後面，修飾及補充說明名詞，舉例來說：work to do就是用不定詞該去完成（to do）形容前面的work，指該完成的工作。

a few
[əˈfju]

片 一些
I have a few messages to listen to.
我有一些留言要聽。

ninety
[ˈnaɪntɪ]

形 九十
My ninety-year-old grandpa has many stories to tell.
我九十歲的爺爺有很多故事可以講。

dry
[draɪ]

形 乾燥 動 弄乾
Do you want me to dry the towel for you?
你想要我幫你把毛巾弄乾嗎？

cent
[sɛnt]

名 分
I have seventy five cents left to spend.
我剩七毛五的錢可以花用。

mile
[maɪl]

名 英里
They still have three miles to go.
他們還有三英里的路程。

5.疑問詞 "to"

2-22

不定詞也可以放在疑問詞後面，來形容疑問詞，表示你不知道有關
於那個不定詞的訊息，舉例來說：what to do後面的不定詞（to do）
用來修飾前面的疑問詞（what），表示不知道要做什麼。

good-bye (goodbye)
[gʊd'baɪ]

名 再見
I don't need to tell him when to say good-bye.
我不需要告訴他何時說再見。

meat
[mit]

名 肉
They have no idea how to cook the meat.
他們完全不知道該怎麼料理肉。

pair
[pɛr]

名 一對；一雙
She didn't tell me where to find the pair of gloves.
她沒跟我說該去哪裡找那雙手套。

excuse
[ɪk'skjuz]

動 原諒
Excuse me. Do you know how to use the computer?
不好意思，你知道怎麼使用這台電腦嗎？

blow
[blo]

動 吹
My sister doesn't know how to blow up a balloon.
我妹妹不知道如何吹氣球。

6.不定詞的否定

不定詞的否定和一般否定一樣，若是句中的動詞是一般動詞，就在動詞前面依照時態和人稱，加上否定助動詞don't、didn't、doesn't，若句中是be動詞，就在be動詞後面接上not。

if
[ɪf]

連 如果

I don't want to know if he's coming.
我不想知道他是否要來。

mailman (mail carrier)
[ˈmelmən]

名 郵差

The mailman doesn't have any mail to give us.
郵差沒有任何信件要給我們。

kite
[kaɪt]

名 風箏

Jack is not happy to lose his new kite
傑克很不開心他弄丟了新風箏。

half
[hæf]

名 一半

Half of us don't want to accept the challenge.
我們之中有一半的人不想接受挑戰。

hot
[ˈhɑtˌdɔg]

形 熱的

Don't you want hot coffee to drink?
你不想要喝些熱咖啡嗎?

7.不定詞當主詞

要跟朋友聊聊做某件事情的甘苦談，可以用不定詞當主詞，針對不定詞引導的那件事發表意見。句子的結構和一般的句子相同《不定詞＋動詞＋受詞》，用來描述不定詞所說明的那件事。

wall
[wɔl]

名 牆壁

To paint the walls is a lot of work.
粉刷牆壁是件大工程。

convenient
[kənˈvinjənt]

形 便利的

To take the MRT is very convenient.
搭捷運很方便。

bad
[bæd]

形 壞的；不好的
To hurt other people is bad.
傷害別人是不好的。

cool
[kul]

形 涼快的；酷
To fight for your dream is really cool!
為夢想奮鬥很酷！

fourteen
[for'tin]

名 十四
To deal with fourteen kids at a time is exhausting.
一次面對十四個小朋友很累人。

8. It is…to

要針對不定詞指的那件事發表意見時，可以用句型《It is+形容詞＋不定詞》。It在這裡是虛主詞，也就是沒有實質意義的主詞，真正的主詞是不定詞。這樣的句型也可以轉換成《不定詞＋is＋形容詞》的形式。

find
[faɪnd]

動 發現
It is urgent to find my child.
找到我的小孩是很緊急的。

comfortable
['kʌmfɚtəbl]

形 舒服的
It is comfortable to sit on that chair.
坐在那張椅子上很舒服。

common
['kɑmən]

形 常見的
It is common to own pets in the U.S.A..
在美國養寵物很普遍。

fun
[fʌn]

名 樂趣 形 有趣的
It was fun to go fishing.
釣魚很好玩。

less
[lɛs]

形 更少的
It is important to eat less and exercise more.
少吃多動很重要。

和前面的句型相同，只是在句中加入《for＋人》，就可以表達出「對某人而言」這個概念，所以《It is＋形容詞＋for＋人＋不定詞》就表示「不定詞這件事對某人來說是…」的意思。

climb
[klaɪm]

動 登山
It isn't hard for me to climb to the top.
對我來說爬到山頂並不困難。

excellent
['ɛksələnt]

形 出色的；極好的
It is lucky for him to have an excellent partner.
對他來說有個出色的夥伴是很幸運的。

cheer
['tʃɪr]

動 喝采
It is pleasing for Jack to hear his friends cheering for him.
對傑克來說聽到朋友為他喝采是很開心的。

stranger
[strendʒ]

名 陌生人
It is bad for you to chat with a stranger.
對你來說和陌生人聊天是不好的。

fall
[fɔl]

動 落下
It is dangerous for the elderly to fall off the chair.
對年長者來說從椅子上摔下是很危險的。

無法答應別人的要求、邀請時，可以用《Too＋形容詞＋不定詞》就是「太…而不能…」，委婉地說出自己的苦衷，來請對方諒解。在句子中加入《for＋人》表示針對某人而言。

push
[pʊʃ]

動 推
I am too tired to push the door open.
我太累了，而沒辦法推開門。

inside
['ɪn'saɪd]

副 在～裡面
He is too fat to hide inside the closet.
他太胖了，無法藏身在衣櫥裡。

knowledge
['nɑlɪdʒ]

名 知識
It is never too late to acquire new knowledge.
學習新知永遠不嫌晚。

cover
['kʌvɚ]

動 蓋住
This sheet is too small to cover the whole bed.
這件床單太小了，無法蓋住整張床。

seventh
['sɛvənθ]

形 第七的
Is she too busy to celebrate Nancy's seventh birthday?
她太忙了，無法慶祝南西的七歲生日嗎？

1.And

2-24

And是對等連接詞，左右兩邊所連接的事物要對稱，要是左邊的是單字，那麼and右邊也必須是單字，若是左邊是動詞片語右邊也必須相同，而且詞性也必須對稱喔，像是名詞對名詞、形容詞對形容詞。

nod
[nɑd]

動 點頭
George and Mary nodded to each other.
喬治跟瑪莉對彼此點頭。

shoulder
['ʃoldɚ]

名 肩膀
Relax your shoulders and your arms.
把你的肩膀和手臂都放鬆下來。

belong
[bɪ'lɔŋ]

動 屬於
The dog and the cat belong to me.
那狗跟貓都是我的。

because
[bɪ'kɔz]

連 因為
I went home and took a shower because I was too tired.
因為我太累了，所以回家然後洗澡。

drop
[drɑp]

動 滴落；放下
Release the girl and drop your weapons!
放開那女孩，放下你的武器！

2.But

2-24

當事情有了變化，語氣有轉折，像是中文裡的「但是、不過、可是」，都可以使用but這個轉折連接詞。和前面的連接詞一樣，but左右所連接的事物要對稱，詞性和類型都要相同，規定和and相似。

shape
[ʃep]

名 形狀

The shape of the cookie is weird but creative.
那餅乾的形狀很奇怪但很有創意。

kilogram
[ˈkɪləgræm]

名 公斤

Fifty kilograms is an OK weight for me but not OK for a model.
五十公斤對我而言很OK，但對模特兒來說不是。

bored
[bord]

副 感到厭煩的

She wanted to cheer up Sam but he felt bored.
她想要取悅山姆，但他覺得很無聊。

kick
[kɪk]

動 踢

I tried to kick the ball but missed it.
我試著踢那顆球但卻失了準頭。

twenty
[ˈtwɛntɪ]

名 二十

There are twenty minutes left but I have five pages still unread.
剩下二十分鐘，我卻還有五頁還沒讀。

3.Or

2-24

選擇餐點、選要買哪件衣服、選擇要唸的科系…，生活上常會面臨大大小小的選擇，Or就是給人選擇的連接詞，左右連接的是對稱的兩個選擇。兩邊的類型、詞性都要相同。

whether
[ˈhwɛðɚ]

連 是否

He doesn't care whether we win or lose.
他不在乎是輸還是贏。

no
[no]

形 沒有；不是

I have no idea which team's better, the Lakers or the Sixers.
我完全不知道湖人隊和七六人隊哪個比較好。

medium
['midɪəm]

形 中的

Please give me a medium size or a small size.
請給我中號的或是小號的。

full
[fʊl]

形 飽了的；充滿的

Is the bag full or empty?
那袋子是滿的還是空的？

wind
[wɪnd]

名 風

Is the wind cold or warm?
風是冷的還是溫暖的？

4.Because放在句中

2-25

要說明原因、解釋狀況的時候，用Because連接主要子句和附屬子句，形成這樣《主要子句＋because＋附屬子句》的結構，其中附屬子句是用來解釋原因，無法跟主要子句分開自成一句。

ruler
['rulɚ]

名 尺

The line wasn't straight because she didn't use a ruler.
這條線不直是因為她沒有用尺（畫）。

friendly
['frɛndlɪ]

形 友善的

The girls like Jason because he is handsome and friendly.
女孩們喜歡傑森，因為他長得帥又很友善。

pound
[paʊnd]

名 磅

The markets here confuse me because they sell things by the pound.
這裡的市場讓我很困惑，因為它們都按磅來賣東西。

post office
['post,ɔfɪs]

名 郵局

The post office is closed today because it's Sunday.
因為今天是星期天所以郵局休息。

left
[lɛft]

名 左邊

I was late because I turned left instead of right at that corner.
我遲到是因為在那個轉角左轉了而沒有右轉。

5.Because放在句首

Because也可以放在句子的開頭，形成這樣《Because＋附屬子句＋，主要子句》的結構，其中because所引導的附屬子句是用來解釋主要子句的原因，而且，要注意用逗點分開兩個句子喔。

hobby
[ˈhɑbɪ]

名 嗜好
Because their hobbies were similar, they became friends.
因為他們興趣相近，所以成為朋友。

point
[pɔɪnt]

動 指著
Because I pointed in the wrong direction, she was lost.
因為我指錯方向，所以她迷路了。

front
[frʌnt]

名 前面；正面
Because he's standing in front of me, I can't see anything!
因為他站在我前面，所以我什麼也看不見！

tenth
[tɛnθ]

形 第十
Because it's the tenth visit to the zoo, he felt bored.
因為這是第十次來動物園了，所以他覺得很無聊。

eighth
[eθ]

形 第八的
Because the office is on the eighth floor, I took the elevator.
因為辦公室在八樓，所以我搭了電梯。

6.So

有因就有果，So就是用來說明結果。so可以放在句子中間，連接主要子句和附屬子句，形成《主要子句＋so＋附屬子句》的結構，其中附屬子句用來說明結果；也可以放在句子的開頭，但要注意用逗點分開兩個句子喔。

price
[praɪs]

名 價格
The price was low so I bought it.
價格很低廉所以我就買了。

seventy
[ˈsɛvəntɪ]

名 七十
There are seventy days left before the wedding so he is nervous.
還有七十天就是婚禮了，所以他很緊張。

nineteen [naɪn'tin]	名 十九 They'll spend nineteen days in Europe so they are packing up. 他們要去歐洲十九天，所以正在打包。
forty ['fɔrtɪ]	名 四十 The sandwich costs forty dollars, so I bought something else. 那三明治要四十塊錢，所以我就買別的了（太貴）。
eleven [ɪ'lɛvən]	名 十一 Lydia just took an eleven-hour flight so she wants to rest. 莉蒂亞剛結束十一小時的航程，所以她想要休息一下。

7.Before

2-26

Before是說明時間先後的連接詞，可以放在句子的中間，形成這樣《主要子句＋before＋附屬子句》的結構（其中附屬子句是用來敘述較早發生的事件），或是放在句子的開頭，只是要注意用逗點分開兩個句子喔。

spend [spɛnd]	動 花費 Think twice before you spend that money. 花那筆錢之前要三思。
ear [ɪr]	名 耳朵 I covered my ears before she started to talk. 在她開始講話之前我就把耳朵蓋起來了。
August ['ɔgəst]	名 八月 We should finish the report before August. 我們應該在八月前完成報告。
sell [sɛl]	動 賣 Before you sell used computers, you should sheck them. 賣二手電腦前你應該要檢查。
guess [gɛs]	動 名 猜測 Before I tell you the answer, why don't you make a guess? 在我告訴你答案之前，何不猜猜看呢？

8.After

After是說明時間的先後的連接詞，可以放在句子的中間，形成這樣《主要子句＋after＋附屬子句》的結構，（其中附屬子句是用來敘述較晚發生的事件），也可以放在句子的開頭，但注意要用逗點分開兩個句子喔。

happen
['hæpən']

動 發生
What happened after I left?
我離開後發生了什麼事？

fill
[fɪl]

動 充滿
Fill the pot with water after you clean it.
清洗完鍋子後在裡面裝水。

or
[ɔr]

連 或是
Should I go home or go swimming after school?
放學之後，我該回家還是去游泳呢？

o'clock
[ə'klɑk]

副 ～點鐘
I will not be here after six o'clock.
六點之後我不會在這裡。

bye-bye
['baɪ']

嘆 再見
After dinner, we said bye-bye to each other and returned home.
晚餐結束之後，我們對彼此說再見然後回家。

9.If

If是說明條件和限制的連接詞，可以放在句子的中間，代表著「如果…，就…」，形成這樣《主要子句＋if＋附屬子句》的結構。（其中附屬子句是用來敘述可能的狀況或要求的條件），也可放在句子開頭，但要用逗點分開兩個句子。

also
['ɔlso']

副 也
If your dad's also coming, please let me know.
如果你父親也要來，請先告訴我。

wrong
[rɔŋ]

形 錯誤的
If that's the wrong answer, I will fail the test.
如果那是錯的答案，我考試就會不及格。

welcome
['wɛlkəm]

形 歡迎
You are welcome if you want to come to my house.
如果你想來我家的話，我很歡迎。

either
['iðɚ]

副 也（不）
If he's not going, I am not going either.
如果他不去，我也不會去。

usually
['juʒʊəlɪ]

副 通常
I usually go jogging in the morning if it doesn't rain.
如果沒下雨的話，我通常會去晨跑。

10.Whether

Whether有著義無反顧的精神，代表著「不論如何…」。可以放在句子的中間，形成這樣《主要子句＋whether＋附屬子句》的結構，其中附屬子句是可能的情況，等於「是否…」的意思。

sick
[sɪk]

形 生病的
I can't tell whether this dog is sick (or not).
我無法分辨這狗是否生病了。

abroad
[ə'brɔd]

副 在（到）國外；名 異國，海外
She is not sure whether she will go abroad (or not).
她不確定是否要出國。

fifty
['fɪftɪ]

名 五十
I still won't buy it whether it's less than fifty dollars (or not).
不管它是否在五十元以下我都不會買。

depend
[dɪ'pɛnd]

動 依靠，依～而定
The result depends on whether we win (or not).
結果得看我們有沒有贏。

asleep
[ə'slip]

形 睡著的；副 進入睡眠狀態
You can't fall asleep whether you're tired (or not).
不論你是否疲倦，都不能睡著。

11.when

When用來連接兩件同時發生的事情。左右都是現在式時，代表著「當⋯，就⋯」，是一種普遍的狀況。放在句中是《主要子句＋when＋附屬子句》的結構。When也可以放在句子的開頭，但要用逗點分開兩個句子。

advice
[əd'vaɪs]

名 忠告，勸告

Listen when somebody gives you advice.
有人給你意見的時候要聽。

decision
[dɪ'sɪʒən]

名 決定，結論

You should be careful when you make a decision.
你在做決定的時候應該要小心。

calm
[kɑm]

形 沈著的，平靜的； 名 平靜

Stay calm when you're in danger.
當你身在危險中時要保持冷靜。

delay
[dɪ'le]

名 延遲，耽擱； 動 延緩，延誤

When things are delayed, David becomes nervous.
事情延誤的時候大衛會變得緊張。

jealous
['dʒɛləs]

形 嫉妒的，吃醋的

When Bob talks to other girls, Anna gets jealous.
鮑柏和其他女生說話時，安娜會吃醋。

12.when動詞過去式

When的左右兩個事件都是過去式時，代表「當⋯，就發生了⋯」，描述過去同時發生的事件。放在句子中形成《主要子句＋when＋附屬子句》的結構。When也可放在句子開頭，但要用逗點分開兩個句子喔。

accident
['æksədənt]

名 意外，災禍

I was shocked when I saw that car accident.
看到那場車禍時我感到很震撼。

describe
[dɪ'skraɪb]

動 描寫，敘述

His face turned red when he described that girl to me.
他向我形容那女孩的時候臉都紅了。

everywhere [ˈɛvrɪˌhwɛr]	副 到處 There was trash everywhere when I arrived home. 我回到家時到處都是垃圾。
especially [əˈspɛʃəlɪ]	副 特別地，格外地 When I talked to the class, I especially mentioned that problem. 我對全班說話的時候，特別提到這個問題。
invent [ɪnˈvɛnt]	動 創造，發明 When the camera was invented, nobody was interested in it. 當相機被發明出來時，沒有人對它感興趣。

13.when動詞現在式

2-28

When引導現在式的附屬子句，連接未來式的主要子句，表達出動作先後的銜接，也就是「現在一完成⋯，就馬上⋯」。放在句中形成《主要子句＋when＋附屬子句》的結構。另外，when放在句子的開頭時，要注意用逗點分開兩個句子喔！

barbecue [ˈbɑrbɪkju]	名 烤肉，烤肉餐館；動 戶外烤肉 We will have a barbecue together when my dad returns. 等我爸回來，我們會一起烤肉。
print [prɪnt]	動 列印，發行；名 印刷品 Connie will print the page when the computer is on. 電腦打開後康尼會列印那一頁。
audience [ˈɔdɪəns]	名 觀眾，閱聽眾 When the audience is ready, the show will begin. 當觀眾準備好時，表演就會開始。
data [ˈdetə]	名 資料，數據 When the data is ready, I'll take it to your office. 資料準備好時，我會把它送到你的辦公室。
shout [ʃaʊt]	動 喊叫，呼喊；名 叫聲 I will start to talk when you stop shouting. 等你們停止大聲喊叫，我就會開始說話。

14. While

While是說明同時發生的連接詞，強調持續了一段時間，可以放在句子的中間作連接，形成這樣《主要子句＋while＋附屬子句》的結構。while放在句子開頭時，要注意用逗點分開兩個句子喔。

explain
[ɪkˈsplen]

動 解釋，說明
He looked at me while explaining what had happened.
他看著我，當他在向我解釋發生什麼事情的時候。

bake
[bek]

動 烘烤，曬黑
The guests arrived while I was baking cookies.
當我在烤餅干時，客人就到了。

soccer
[ˈsɑkə]

名 足球
The phone rang while I was watching the soccer game.
我看足球賽的時候電話響了。

memory
[ˈmɛmərɪ]

名 回憶，記憶
While Penny thinks of the old memories, she feels happy.
佩妮想著以前的回憶會很快樂。

tear
[tɪr]

名 眼淚
While she apologized, I saw tears in her eyes.
她道歉的時候，我看見她眼裡有淚光。

15. Not…but

想要澄清誤會、或解釋說明事實時，可以用《Not…but》兩個連接詞組成的組合連接詞，代表「不是…而是…」的意思，同樣的not和but後面接的詞必須詞性和類型都要對稱。

quiz
[kwɪz]

名 測驗，提問
This is not a practice but a quiz..
這不是練習，而是測驗。

realize
[ˈrɪəˌlaɪz]

動 領悟，實現
We realized that she's not angry but upset.
我們發現她沒有生氣，只是沮喪。

super [ˈsupɚ]	形 極度的；副 超級地，極度地 He is not just nice but super nice. 他不只是人好，而是超級好。
receive [rɪˈsiv]	動 接收，收到 He received not a hat but a cup. 他收到的不是帽子，而是個杯子。
snowy [snoɪ]	形 下雪的，多雪的 It is not rainy but snowy. 現在不是下雨，而是下雪。

16.both A and B

2-29

《both A and B》是由兩個連接詞組成的組合連接詞，代表「A和B都」的意思，其實就是and的句型，加上了both來加強語氣，意思用法還是很類似，both和and後面接的詞語需要對稱。

ability [əˈbiliti]	名 能力，才能 Both you and I have the ability to do that. 你跟我都有能力可以做那件事。
Thanksgiving [ˌθæŋksˈgɪvɪŋ]	名 感恩節 Both Thanksgiving and Christmas are important holidays. 感恩節和聖誕節都是重要的節日。
intelligent [ɪnˈtɛlədʒənt]	形 聰明的，有才智的 I am both intelligent and athletic. 我不但聰明也很有運動細胞。
wallet [ˈwɑlɪt]	名 皮夾 She bought both the shoes and the wallet. 她買了鞋子也買了皮夾。
subway [ˈsʌbˌwe]	名 地下鐵，地下道 I ran into Jack both in the library and on the subway 我在圖書館跟體育館都遇到傑克。

要誇讚某人能力很好，可以用《Not only···, but also···》這個組合連接詞，代表「不只···，還···」的意思，後面都要接對稱的語詞，另外，also可以省略。

terrible
['tɛrəbl̩]
形 麻煩的，可怕的
The scandals are not only terrible, but also shameful.
那些醜聞不只是糟糕，也很丟臉。

brave
[brev]
形 勇敢的，英勇的
Louis is not only smart, but also brave.
路易士不只聰明，也很勇敢。

steal
[stil]
動 偷竊，行竊
Paris not only lied, but also stole.
芭莉絲不只撒謊，還偷了東西。

bill
[bɪl]
名 帳單，法案
I not only took him to dinner, but also paid the bill.
我不只帶他去吃晚餐，還付了帳單。

turkey
['tɝkɪ]
名 火雞，火雞肉
They cooked not only potatoes but also turkey.
他們不只煮了馬鈴薯，還有火雞。

18.So···that

2-29

要說明原因和結果的關係時，可以用《So···that》這個組合連接詞，是「太···，以致於···」的意思，其中，so後面可以接上形容詞或副詞，用來表示原因；而that則是引導了一個句子，表示結果。

stick
[stɪk]
名 枝條，棍棒
His mother was so mad that she hit him with a stick.
他母親很生氣，（以致於）用棍子打他。

beard
[bɪrd]
名 鬍鬚
His beard was so long that he looked like an old man.
他的鬍子太長了，（以致於）看起來像個老人。

embarrass
[ɪmˈbærəs]

動 使～不好意思，使～困窘

She was so embarrassesd that she left immediately.
她覺得很尷尬，（以致於）立刻就離開了。

storm
[stɔrm]

名 風暴，暴風雨

The storm was so scary that we all stayed home.
暴風雨太嚇人了，（以致於）我們全部待在家裡。

total
[ˈtotl]

形 總計的；名 合計；動 計算總數

The total price was so high that she couldn't afford it.
總金額太高了，（以致於）她負擔不起。

19.So am I

2-30

想要表示同感時，除了可以用also、too表示「也…」，還可以用
《So＋be動詞＋人》來表示，其中的so就是代替了主要子句，使用
方法是《主要子句＋and＋(So+ be動詞+人)》。

absent
[ˈæbsn̩t]

形 缺席的，不存在的

Jack was absent yesterday and so was I.
傑克昨天缺席，而我也是。

against
[əˈgɛnst]

介 反對，違反

I am against this idea and so are they.
我反對這個想法，而他們也是。

Taiwanese
[ˌtaɪwəˈniz]

形 台灣的，台灣人的；名 台灣人

Linda is a Taiwanese singer and so is Jack.
琳達是一位台灣歌手，而傑克也是。

brunch
[brʌntʃ]

名 早午餐

Kate is used to eating brunch and so is the boss.
凱特習慣吃早午餐，而老闆也是。

shark
[ˈʃark]

名 鯊魚

Dolly is afraid of the sharks, and so is she.
桃莉怕鯊魚，而她也是。

20.So do I

想要告訴對方自己也有同感時，除了可以用also、too表示「也…」，還可以用《主要子句＋and＋(So+ do+人)》來表示，就等於（主要子句＋and＋人＋do, too），其中，若是人是單數就要把do改成does。

accept
[əkˈsɛpt]

動 接受，認可
He accepted my apology and so did she.
他接受了我的道歉，而她也是。

equal
[ˈikwəl]

形 相當的；動 等於；名 同等的人事物
Jerry believes that all men are equal and so do we.
傑瑞相信人都是平等的，而我們也這麼想。

energy
[ˈɛnɚdʒɪ]

名 精力，能量
Emily needs more energy and so do I.
艾蜜莉需要更多的精力，而我也是。

toast
[tost]

名 土司，烤土司；動 烤
Alice loves toast with butter and so does Jason.
艾莉絲很喜歡奶油吐司，而傑森也是。

village
[ˈvɪlɪdʒ]

名 村莊
I prefer small villages to big cities, and so does she.
我喜歡小鎮勝過大城市，而她也是。

21.So can I

想要告訴對方自己也可以做得到，除了可以用also、too表示「也能…」，還可以用《主要子句＋and＋(So+ can+人)》來表示，，其中的so就是代替了主要子句，所以等於（主要子句＋and＋人＋can, too）。

survive
[səˈvaɪv]

動 殘留，倖存
Larry can survive the war and so can I.
賴瑞能在戰爭中活下來，而我也能。

deal
[dil]

動 處理，分配；名 交易
You can deal with it and so can he.
你能處理這件事，而他也能。

volleyball ['vɑlɪ,bɔl]	名 排球，排球運動 Patty can play volleyball well and so can you. 派蒂排球打得很好，而你也能。
support [sə'port]	名 支持，贊助；動 支持 They can support you and so can we. 他們可以支持你，而我們也可以。
yummy ['jʌmɪ]	形 可口的，好吃的，美味的 Ricky can make yummy muffins and so can Lily. 瑞奇會做好吃的杯子蛋糕，而莉莉也能。

22.Neither

2-31

想要告訴對方自己也有同樣負面、否定的感覺時，可以用Neither，代表「也不」的意思，句子結構是《主要子句＋and＋(neither…人)》，和《so…人》的用法相同，只是意思完全相反。

tip [tɪp]	名 提示；動 覆蓋～的尖端 Neither Sally nor Jane wanted to share their cooking tips. 莎莉和珍都不想分享她們烹飪的小秘訣。
design [dɪ'zaɪn]	名 計畫，設計；動 設計 He didn't like that design and neither did Jack. 他不喜歡那個設計，而傑克也不喜歡。
empty ['ɛmptɪ]	形 空的；動 讓～變成空的 That jar is not empty, and neither is the one next to it. 這罐子不是空的，而它旁邊的（罐子）也不是。
waste [west]	名 浪費；動 浪費，消耗 Wendy never wastes money, and neither do I. 溫蒂絕不浪費錢，而我也不。
supper ['sʌpɚ]	名 晚餐，晚飯 Dad hasn't had supper and neither has Mom. 爸爸還沒吃晚餐，而媽媽也還沒。

Too是「也是」的意思，句子結構是《主要子句＋and＋（人＋助動詞/ be動詞）＋ ,too》，口語中常用的Me, too.（我也是），雖不符合文法，但卻常被掛在嘴邊。

koala
[ko'ɑlə]

名 無尾熊
Lucy likes koalas, and Kim does, too.
露西喜歡無尾熊，而金也喜歡。

trick
[trɪk]

名 惡作劇，花招；動 哄騙
He knows a lot of magic tricks, and I do, too.
他知道很多魔術技法，而我也是。

homesick
['hom,sɪk]

形 思鄉病的，想家的
Mathew is homesick, and Lisa is, too.
馬修想家，而麗莎也是。

lovely
['lʌvlɪ]

形 可愛的，美好的
She is a lovely girl, and you are, too.
她是個可人的女孩，而妳也是。

weekday
['wik,de]

名 週間，平日，工作日
She is busy during weekdays, and Diana is, too
她在平日都很忙，而黛安娜也是。

想要告訴對方自己也有同樣負面、否定的感覺、或說到彼此同樣沒做到⋯，Either是「也不是」的意思，意義和too完全相反，但用法和too完全相同。

Walkman
['wɔkmən]

名 隨身聽
I don't use a Walkman anymore, and Patrick doesn't either.
我不再用隨身聽了，而派翠克也不用。

secretary
['sɛkrə,tɛrɪ]

名 祕書，祕書長
Tiffany doesn't have a secretary, and Oliver doesn't either.
蒂芬妮沒有秘書，而奧立弗也沒有。

decorate
['dɛkə'ret']
動 裝飾，佈置，修飾
They didn't decorate the Christmas tree, and we didn't either.
他們沒有裝飾聖誕樹，而我們也沒有。

downstairs
[,daʊn'stɛrz']
形 在樓下，往樓下; 形 樓下的
She wasn't downstairs, and he wasn't either.
她當時不在樓下，而他也不在。

selfish
['sɛlfɪʃ]
形 自私的，只顧自己的
Cathy is not a selfish person, and Frank isn't either.
凱希不是個自私的人，而法蘭克也不是。

25. either…or…

想法不確定時，就用《either…or…》這組合連接詞，說出「不是…就是…」代表自己有隱約的記憶。和前面連接詞相同，either和or後面接的詞語必須對稱，詞性和類型必須相同。

suggest
[sə'dʒɛst']
動 建議，提議
I suggest you play either basketball or tennis.
我建議你不是打籃球，就是打網球。

wedding
['wɛdɪŋ]
名 結婚典禮，婚禮
The wedding will be either this month or next.
婚禮不是這個月舉行，就是下個月。

honey
['hʌnɪ]
名 蜂蜜；甜蜜
You may choose either jam or honey.
你有果醬和蜂蜜可以二選一。

dentist
['dɛntɪst']
名 牙醫
Either Jack or I will take her to the dentist.
不是傑克就是我將帶她去看牙醫。

suit
[sut]
動 適用於，適合
Either you or he suits our needs.
不是你就是他符合我們的需求。

26.neither…nor…

2-32

一時忘記正確答案，可以用刪去法，把不對的選項去掉，《neither
…nor…》這組合連接詞，有著「既不…也不…」的刪去概念。 而
neither和or後面接的詞語同樣必須對稱，詞性和類型也必須相同。

dolphin
['dalfɪn]

名 海豚
I don't see any whales nor dolphins here.
這裡我看不到有任何鯨魚或是海豚。

pumpkin
['pʌmpkɪn]

名 南瓜
Joy likes neither pumpkin pie nor apple pie.
喬依不想要南瓜派，也不想要蘋果派。

duck
[dʌk]

名 鴨，鴨肉
I want neither chicken nor duck.
我既不想要雞肉，也不想要鴨肉。

Europe
['jʊrəp]

名 歐洲
Neither Lily nor I have been to Europe.
莉莉和我都沒去過歐洲。

direction
[də'rɛkʃən]

名 方向，領導
Neither you nor he knows the right direction.
你和他都不知道正確的方向。

1.With後接名詞（1）

2-33

出去遊玩、旅行最重要的就是隨行的伙伴了，可以用with說說自己
是跟誰一夥的。With是「和」的意思，後面可以接名詞，《with＋一
起行動的人或物》就變成「和某人或某物一起」。

suddenly
['sʌdn̩lɪ]

副 突然地，忽然
He suddenly showed up with the boss.
他和老闆忽然一起現身。

magazine
[ˌmæɡə'zin]

名 雜誌，期刊
Lisa is reading magazines with Mark.
麗莎正和馬克一起看雜誌。

Russia
['rʌʃə]

名 俄羅斯
Patty moved to Russia with her husband.
派蒂和她丈夫一起搬到俄國住。

Valentine's Day
['væləntaɪnz de]

名 情人節
Dolly had dinner with Miller on Valentine's Day.
情人節那天桃莉和米勒一起吃晚餐。

roof
[ruf]

名 屋頂，頂部
Rita climbed onto the roof with her little brother.
麗塔和弟弟一起爬上屋頂。

2.without後接名詞（2）

2-33

Without是「沒有…」的意思，後面可以接名詞，《with＋人或物》就變成「沒有和某人或某物一起」。

whole
[hol]

形 全部的；名 全部，整體
This family is not whole without you.
這個家沒有你是不完整的。

handle
['hændl]

動 處理，搬動
Kate can handle the report without any partners.
凱特沒有任何夥伴就可以處理這個報告。

emotion
[ɪ'moʃən]

名 情感，情緒，感情
I told the truth without personal emotion.
我不帶私人感情地說出真相。

roll
[rol]

動 滾動；名 捲餅，捲狀物
Wendy made some egg rolls without sugar.
溫蒂做了些沒放糖的蛋捲。

weight
[wet]

名 重，重量
You can't lose weight without exercise.
你不能不運動就減重。

3.without後接名詞（3）

Without是「沒有」的意思，後面若是要接動作時，要把動詞變成動名詞的型態，《without＋沒有發生的事》就變成「沒有…」。

discuss
[dɪˈskʌs]

動 討論，商討
Jack made the decision without discussing it with his wife.
傑克沒有和他妻子討論就做了決定。

underwear
[ˈʌndɚˌwɛr]

名 內衣
You can't go to school without wearing underwear!
妳不能不穿內衣就去學校！

Korea
[koˈriə]

名 韓國
We went to Korea without telling our parents.
我們沒跟父母說就去了韓國。

likely
[ˈlaɪklɪ]

形 可能的，適合的；副 很可能
It is very likely that he left home without closing the door.
他很可能沒有關門就離開家了。

customer
[ˈkʌstəmɚ]

名 顧客，買主，消費者
You can't run a business without understanding customers.
做生意不能不了解顧客。

1.一般動詞用法

附加問句是在直述句後，接上簡短的問句並用逗號隔開。若直述句是肯定的，後面問句就是否定的。否定助動詞要用縮寫形式，如：doesn't、can't…；直述句是否定的，後面附加問句是肯定的。

diary
[ˈdaɪərɪ]

名 日誌，日記
You keep a diary, don't you?
你有寫日記（的習慣），對吧？

power
[ˈpauɚ]

名 權力，電力，力量
She has great power, doesn't she?
她有很大的權力，對吧？

judge
[dʒʌdʒ]

名 法官，裁判；動 評判
The judge believes me, doesn't he?
法官相信我，對吧？

Halloween
[ˌhælo'in]

名 萬聖節
We have to celebrate Halloween, don't we?
我們一定得慶祝萬聖節，對吧？

haircut
['hɛrˌkʌt]

名 理髮
Jack needs a haircut, doesn't he?
傑克需要剪頭髮，對吧？

2.Be動詞用法

2-34

be動詞的附加問句，如果直述句是肯定的，那麼後面要加上否定的附加問句（否定be動詞＋人），否定be動詞都要用縮寫形式，如：aren't、isn't、wasn't…；如果直述句是否定的，那麼後面加上的附加問句就是肯定的（be動詞＋人）。

diet
['daɪət]

名 飲食，食物；動 節食
They are on a diet, aren't they?
他們在節食，是嗎？

semester
[sə'mɛstɚ]

名 一學期，半學年
This semester is finished, isn't it?
這學期已經結束了，對吧？

level
['lɛvl]

名 程度；形 水平的，同高度的
The level of this book is too difficult, isn't it?
這本書的程度太困難了，是吧？

kindergarten
['kɪndɚˌgɑrtn]

名 幼稚園
They are kindergarten teachers, aren't they?
他們是幼稚園老師，是吧？

distance
['dɪstəns]

名 距離，路程
It's a long distance, isn't it?
距離很遠，是嗎？

1.現在分詞形容詞―放在名詞後

靈活使用動詞轉變成的形容詞，可以讓描述的人事物更多了一分生動。現在分詞當作形容詞使用時，位置可以放在名詞後面，用來修飾形容名詞。表示「正在…就是…」。

huge
[hjudʒ]
形 龐大的，巨大的
The dog running over here is huge!
跑過來的那隻狗好大啊!

horrible
[ˈhɔrəbḷ]
形 可怕的，令人毛骨悚然的
The movie playing now is horrible.
現在正在播放的電影很可怕。

Teacher's Day
[ˈtitʃɚs de]
形 教師節
The day after tomorrow is Teacher's Day.
明天過後到來的是教師節。

curious
[ˈkjʊrɪəs]
形 好奇的，愛探究的
The boy sitting there seems to be curious about us.
坐在那裡的男孩似乎對我們很好奇。

hi
[haɪ]
嘆 嗨（問候語）
Hi! Is the cell phone ringing yours?
嗨！是你的手機在響嗎?

2.現在分詞形容詞―放在名詞前

靈活使用動詞轉變成的形容詞，可以讓描述的人事物更多了一分生動。現在分詞當作形容詞使用時，位置也可以在名詞前面，用來修飾形容名詞。表示「正在…就是…」。

leaf
[lif]
名 葉子
We like those falling leaves.
我們很喜歡那些正落下的葉子。

impossible
[ɪmˈpasəbḷ]
形 不可能的，辦不到的
It's impossible for her to see the flying bird.
她不可能看得到在飛的鳥兒。

164

shake
[ʃek]
動 搖動，握手；名 搖動
I can't stand the plane shaking.
我受不了飛機一直搖晃。

thief
[θif]
名 賊，小偷
They can't catch the running thief
她們抓不到那個逃跑的小偷。

rise
[raɪz]
動 升起
David loves the rising Sun.
大衛很喜歡升起的太陽。

3.過去分詞形容詞－放在名詞後

2-35

靈活使用動詞轉變成的形容詞，讓描述的對象更生動。現在分詞當作形容詞使用時，位置也可以在名詞後面，而要形容的名詞不是自己進行動作，而是被動地接受那個動作。表示「被…就是…」。

protect
[prə'tɛkt]
動 保護，防護
This is the girl protected by the police.
這個女孩是警方在保護的。

crowd
[kraʊd]
名 人群，群眾
The crowd was gathered by the speaker.
那群眾是由演講者招集的。

recycle
[ri'saɪkl]
動 再利用，再循環，回收
These are the bottles that are recycled.
這些是回收的瓶子。

provide
[prə'vaɪd]
動 提供，供給
These are the cars provided by Ford.
這些是福特提供的車子。

choose
[tʃuz]
動 選擇，挑選
This is the gift chosen by Sarah.
這是莎拉挑選的禮物。

4.過去分詞形容詞—放在名詞前

靈活使用動詞轉變成的形容詞,可以讓描述的對象更生動。現在分詞當作形容詞使用時,位置也可以在名詞後面,而要形容的名詞不是自己進行動作,而是被動地接受那個動作。表示「被…就是…」。

melon
['mɛlən]

名 香瓜,甜瓜
Try some sliced melon.
來試試切片的香瓜。

robot
['robət]

名 機器人,自動控制機器
Let's see the newly invented robot.
我們來瞧瞧這新發明的機器人吧。

rob
[rɑb]

動 搶劫,盜掠
We're talking about the robbed gold.
我們正在討論被搶走的金子。

toothbrush
['tuθ,brʌʃ]

名 牙刷
Don't use that broken toothbrush.
別用那支壞掉的牙刷。

across
[ə'krɔs]

介 穿過;副 在對面
The newly opened store is across the street.
那家新開的店面位在對街。

1.未來式

be going to後面接上動詞原型,可以用來表示未來將要發生的動作、行為,屬於比較輕鬆、不一定會達成的未來計畫,語氣沒有will那麼堅決。

France
[fræns]

名 法國
We are going to visit our grandparents in France.
我們將要去拜訪在法國的祖父母。

forward
['fɔrwəd]

副 向前,今後;形 前面的
I am going to move forward.
我要往前移動。

prize
[praɪz]

名 獎品，獎賞
Mary is going to win the big prize!
瑪莉要拿到那個大獎了！

prince
[prɪns]

名 王子，國君
You are going to be a prince in the future.
你將來會是個王子。

mall
[mɔl]

名 購物中心
He is going to the mall after lunch.
他在午餐過後要去購物商場。

2.未來式疑問句（1）

2-36

be going to的疑問句，就是把直述句中的be動詞移到句首，其餘的都不變，變成《be動詞＋人＋going to＋未來將要做的事》，用來詢問未來的計畫。回答是用yes、no來開頭。

skate
[sket]

名 溜冰鞋，溜冰；動 溜冰
Are they going to go skating together?
他們要一起去溜冰嗎？

sign
[saɪn]

動 簽名，簽署，寫下
Is he going to sign the contract tomorrow?
他明天會簽合約嗎？

slippers
['slɪpɚ]

名 拖鞋，室內拖鞋
Are you going to wear slippers?
你打算要穿拖鞋嗎？

fool
[ful]

名 傻瓜；形 愚蠢的；動 欺騙
Is he going to fool the professor?
他打算要欺騙教授嗎？

apologize
[ə'pɑlə,dʒaɪz]

動 道歉，認錯
Are they going to apologize to me?
他們要向我道歉嗎？

3.未來式疑問句（2）

be going to的疑問句，可以針對想問的是：什麼人、用什麼方法、什麼時候…，來加上疑問詞who、how、when…。句型《疑問詞＋be＋人＋going to＋未來的計畫》，可詢問未來將要發生的事。

poster [post]	名 海報，公告 What are you going to do with the poster? 你要怎麼處理那張海報？
century ['sɛntʃʊrɪ]	名 世紀 What's going to be popular in the next century? 下個世紀會流行什麼？
prove [pruv]	動 證明，證實 How are you going to prove it? 你要怎麼證明？
mine [maɪn]	代 我的東西 Are these going to be mine? 這些會成為我的東西嗎？
tiny ['taɪnɪ]	形 微小的，極小的 Who is going to see that tiny mistake? 誰會看到那極小的錯誤呢？

4.未來式否定句

Be going to的否定句，是在be和going to中間，加上否定詞not，變成《人＋be動詞＋not＋going to＋未來沒要做的事》，用來表達未來沒有要做的事。

diamond ['daɪəmənd]	名 鑽石 We are not going to buy the diamond. 我們不會買那個鑽石。
salesman ['selzmən]	名 業務員，推銷員 I am not going to be a salesman. 我不會成為一個業務員。

Japan
[dʒə'pæn]

名 日本
I am not going to live in Japan.
我不是要住在日本。

plant
[plænt]

動 栽種，種植
He is not going to plant a tree in the backyard.
他不是要在後院種樹。

shut
[ʃʌt]

動 關上，合攏
We are not going to shut up.
我們沒有要閉嘴。

1.Will you

2-37

想要委婉地請對方幫忙、或提出邀請，可以使用《Will you＋請求事項？》這樣的句型，其中的you可以依照對象的不同而更改。而請求事項裡的動詞，一定要使用原型。

argue
['ɑrgjʊ]

動 爭論，主張
Will you stop arguing with me?—Sure.
你可以停止和我爭辯嗎？—好阿。

certainly
['sɝtənlɪ]

副 無疑地，確實，當然
Will you call me later?—Certainly.
你可以等一下打給我嗎？—沒問題。

silent
['saɪlənt]

動 沈默的，寂靜無聲的
Will you please keep silent?—Sorry.
你可以保持安靜嗎？—抱歉。

dessert
[dɪ'zɝt]

名 點心，飯後甜點
Will you pass me the dessert?—OK.
你可以把甜點傳給我嗎？—好。

alone
[ə'lon]

副 單獨地；形 獨自的
Will you please leave me alone?—All right.
你可以讓我一個人靜一靜嗎？—好吧。

2.Shall I

想要開口詢問對方需不需要幫忙、或是客氣的詢問自己能不能做某件事時，可以使用《Shall I＋詢問事項？》這樣的句型，其中詢問事項裡一定要使用原型動詞。

rope
[rop]
名 繩子
Shall I pass you the rope?—Yes, please.
要不要我把繩子傳給你嗎？—好啊，麻煩你。

toilet
['tɔɪlɪt]
名 廁所，洗手間
Shall I help you clean the toilet?—No, thank you.
要不要我幫你一起打掃廁所？—不了，謝謝。

beginning
[bɪ'ɡɪnɪŋ]
名 開端；形 開始的，起源的
Shall I start from the beginning?—Yes, thank you.
要不要我重頭開始？—謝謝。

tool
[tul]
名 工具，用具
Shall I find more tools for you?—Yes, please.
要不要現在幫你找其他工具？好啊。

bit
[bɪt]
名 小塊，小量，一會兒
Shall I get a little bit of wine for you?—No, thank you.
要不要我幫你拿一些酒來？—不了，謝謝。

3.Shall we

想要提出邀請、要求對方一起時，可以說《Shall we＋邀請內容》。在shall we前面加上疑問詞，例如：《When shall we…?》（我們什麼時候…？），來詢問對方各式各樣關於「我們…」的話題。

area
['ɛrɪə]
名 面積，區域
Shall we meet in that area?
我們要在那塊地方會面嗎？

Asia
['eʃə]
名 亞洲
How shall we get to Asia?
我們要怎麼到亞洲去？

tie
[taɪ]

名 領帶，結
Which tie shall I wear?
我要戴哪條領帶？

basement
[ˈbesmənt]

名 地下室
What shall I leave in the basement?
我要在地下室留下什麼東西？

topic
[ˈtɑpɪk]

名 主題，題目
When shall we change the topic?
我們什麼時候換個話題？

1.動名詞一當補語

2-38

一個句子裡只能有一個動詞，所以當出現了兩個動作時，後面的動詞要變成動名詞，當作前面動詞的補語，才不會造成兩動詞同時出現的文法錯誤。

chess
[tʃɛs]

名 西洋棋
He stopped playing chess.
他停止下棋了。

tail
[tel]

名 尾巴，尾部
The dog started chasing its own tail.
那隻狗開始追自己的尾巴。

attention
[əˈtɛnʃən]

名 注意，注意力
Try paying attention, please.
請專心點。

puppy
[ˈpʌpɪ]

名 小狗狗，幼犬
I like playing with the puppy.
我喜歡和小狗玩。

childhood
[ˈtʃaɪldˌhʊd]

名 幼年時期，童年時期
He enjoys talking about his childhood.
他很喜歡談他的童年。

2.動名詞—當主詞

動名詞因為具有名詞的性質，所以也可以放在句首當作主詞，《動名詞＋be動詞＋形容語句》，用這樣的句型就可以形容說明某項行為。

main
[men]

形 主要的，首要的
Meeting new friends is the main reason (why) he came.
認識新朋友是他來這裡的主要原因。

row
[ro]

名 列，排
Standing in rows would be better.
站成一排一排的會比較好。

poem
['poɪm]

名 詩
Writing a poem is difficult for me.
寫詩對我來說很困難。

necessary
['nɛsə,sɛrɪ]

形 必要的，必需的，必然的
Respecting one another is necessary.
尊重他人是十分必要的。

midnight
['mɪd,naɪt]

名 午夜，半夜；形 半夜的
Burning the midnight oil is bad for your health.
熬夜對身體不好。

1.Both放句首，在動詞前面

想要描述兩個有相同狀況的對象時，可以用both，一次針對兩者同時說明：《Both of＋複數受格＋敘述內容》或《Both＋對象1 and對象2＋敘述內容》，而既然是兩個對象，後面動詞當然是複數型囉！

alive
[ə'laɪv]

形 活著的，有活力的
Both of the dogs are alive.
兩隻狗都活著的。

beat
[bit]

動 打，打敗；名 拍子
Both of the teams were beaten.
兩支隊伍都被打敗了。

172

available
[ə'veləbḷ]

形 可獲得的，可用的，有效的
Both of these CDs are available.
這兩片CD都還買得到。

beginner
[bɪ'gɪnɚ]

名 初學者
Both of the twins are beginners.
兩個雙胞胎都是初學者。

throughout
[θru'aʊt]

介 遍及，偏佈，貫穿
Both of them are famous throughout the world.
他們兩個都是世界知名的。

2. Both放句中，在動詞後面

◎
2-39

both用來描述的是兩個有相同狀況的對象時，也可以放在動詞後面：《對象1 and對象2＋動詞＋both＋敘述內容》，現在式時動詞用are或動詞原型即可。

badminton
['bædmɪntən]

名 羽毛球
Ricky and I are both fond of badminton.
瑞奇和我都喜歡打羽毛球。

bench
[bɛntʃ]

名 長椅，長凳
Sam and Lisa both sat on the bench.
山姆和麗莎都坐在長凳上。

AIDS
[edz]

名 後天免疫不健全症（愛滋病）
They both have AIDS.
他們兩人都有愛滋病。

advance
[əd'væns]

名 預先的，前進；動 促進
We both studied in advance.
我們兩個都事先讀過了。

bother
['bɑðɚ]

動 打擾，擔心；名 煩惱
You both should stop bothering me.
你們兩個都該停止打擾我了。

當要說明的對象是三者以上的全體時，就會用all來涵蓋全部的範圍。用法和both很像：《All of＋對象＋敘述內容》。既然是三者以上，後面動詞當然也是複數型囉！

attack
[əˈtæk]

名 攻擊；動 進攻，責難
All of the cities were attacked.
所有的城市都被攻擊了。

active
[ˈæktɪv]

形 活潑的，積極的；名 積極的人
All of the players are active.
所有的選手都很積極。

bat
[bæt]

名 球棒（拍），蝙蝠；動 打球
All of the bats are broken.
所有的棒子都斷了。

cage
[kedʒ]

名 鳥籠
All of the birds are in the cage.
所有的鳥都在籠子裡。

attend
[əˈtɛnd]

動 出席，前往
All of the members attended the meeting.
所有的成員都出席了會議。

4.全部不可數—All

2-40

all用來涵蓋全部的範圍，句型和前面一樣，但要注意動詞用法喔！當對象是不可數名詞時，Be動詞和一般動詞都要做《第三人稱‧單數》的變化，例如：walk→walks、are→is。

information
[ˌɪnfɚˈmeʃən]

名 資訊，報導，情報
All of the information is gone.
所有的情報都不見了。

furniture
[ˈfɝnɪtʃɚ]

名 傢俱
All of the furniture is hand-made.
所有的傢俱都是手工打造。

cancel
[ˈkænsl̩]

動 刪去，取消
All of the work was canceled.
所有的工作都取消了。

cafeteria
[ˌkæfəˈtɪrɪə]

名 自助餐館
All of the food in this cafeteria is delicious.
這家自助餐廳的所有食物都很好吃。

generous
[ˈdʒɛnərəs]

形 慷慨的，大方的
The generous man took out all of his money.
那慷慨的男士拿出了他所有的錢。

5.人或事物中的一部份

當描述的對象是人或事物中的一部份時，會用《數量＋of＋對象＋描述內容》的句型。描述部分的範圍，依照數量的不同有大有小，例如：one（之一）、some（其中有些）、most（其中大部分）…。

article
['ɑrtɪkl̩]
名 文章，論文
One of the articles is mine.
文章之中有一篇是我的。

Australia
[ɔ'streljə]
名 澳大利亞（澳洲）
Some of the girls came from Australia.
有些女孩是從澳洲來的。

button
['bʌtn̩]
名 鈕扣，按鈕；動 扣上
Many of the buttons are red.
有好幾個鈕扣是紅色的。

bone
[bon]
名 骨頭，骨骼
Several of the bones heve to be checked.
有很多骨頭要被檢查。

avoid
[ə'vɔɪd]
動 避開，避免；[同]keep away from; [反]face up
Most of us want to avoid rush hour.
我們之中大部分的人都想避開尖峰時間。

6.兩者之一——One of

沒有要給予確定的選擇時，可以用one of來將想說的對象限定在二選一的範圍內。要注意喔！因為one of是指兩者之一，所指對象是單數的一人，所以，後面接的動詞要用《第三人稱‧單數》喔！

aware
[ə'wɛr]
形 知道的，察覺的
One of us was aware of his madness.
我們其中之一有人察覺到他的忿怒。

blood
[blʌd]
名 血液，血統
One of the blood samples is type B.
兩（個）血液樣本有一個是B型。

gentle
['dʒɛntl̩]

形 溫和的，輕輕的
One of the boys is gentle.
兩個男孩其中的一位很溫和。

later
['letɚ]

副 稍後
One of the bags will be taken later.
其中的一個包包晚一點會被拿走。

purchase
['pɝtʃəs]

名 購買，買；動 購買
She purchased one of the books.
她買了其中一本書。

1.使役動詞―後接形容詞

2-41

使役動詞就是「某人使另外一人…」，最常見的使役動詞就是make（讓），如果是讓某人心情改變的話，就可以直接用《人1＋make＋人2＋心情的形容詞》，其中人1若是單數，make加s。

gentleman
['dʒɛntl̩mən]

名 紳士，男士
The gentleman wished us luck.
那位紳士祝福我們好運。

greedy
['gridɪ]

形 貪吃的，貪婪的
The greedy kids made their parents crazy.
貪吃的孩子們讓他們的父母快抓狂。

actor
['æktɚ]

名 演員，行動者
The director asked the actor to be angry.
導演要求演員生氣。

genius
['dʒinjəs]

名 天賦，天才
That genius makes me envious.
那個天才讓我感到忌妒。

citizen
['sɪtəzn̩]

名 市民
"I wish the citizens were happy!" said the mayor.
「我希望市民都快樂！」市長說。

2.使役動詞—後接動詞原型

2-41

使役動詞也可以用在命令、要求,《人1＋使役動詞＋人2＋動詞》,像是:「某人要求另外一人做⋯」、「某人叫另外一人去⋯」,要注意喔!這時後面接的是原型動詞。

cereal
['sɪrɪəl]

名 麥片,穀類植物
Mom let him have cereal with milk.
母親讓他吃麥片配牛奶。

carpet
['kɑrpɪt]

名 地毯
My sister helped me clean the carpet.
我姐姐幫我清理地毯。

channel
['tʃænl]

名 頻道,航道,途徑
Nicky has his brother change the channel.
尼奇叫他弟弟轉台。

carrot
['kærət]

名 胡蘿蔔
Mom made me finish the carrots.
母親叫我吃完那些胡蘿蔔。

chapter
['tʃæptɚ]

名 章節
The teacher had her read the whole chapter.
老師叫她朗讀一整個章節。

3.感官(知覺)動詞後接原型動詞<表示事實、狀態>

2-41

感官動詞就是用「五覺」感受的動作,像是:視覺(see)、聽覺(hear)、嗅覺(smell)、體覺(feel)⋯等,形成《感官動詞＋人或物＋動作》的句型。注意喔!要用原型動詞來表示你感覺到的事實或存在的狀態。

calendar
['kæləndɚ]

名 日曆,行事曆
I saw my dad hanging up the calendar.
我看見我父親在掛日曆。

clap
[klæp]

動 拍手,輕拍;名 拍手聲
She heard the audience clap.
她聽見觀眾在鼓掌。

granddaughter
['græn,dɔtɚ]

名 孫女，外孫女

I listened to the grandpa talk to his granddaughter.
我聽到祖父在跟他孫女說話。

ghost
[gost]

名 鬼，鬼魂

He felt a ghost touching him
他感覺到一個鬼魂在觸碰他。

ceiling
['silɪŋ]

名 天花板

They saw water dropping from the ceiling.
他們看到水從天花板滴下來。

4.感官（知覺）動詞後接動名詞<表示動作正在進行>

2-42

想要生動地傳達出你的體驗，讓你的朋友也有身歷其境的臨場真實感，可以使用動名詞，當作感官動詞後的動作，用來強調動態的進行，如此一來，可以讓你描述的動作就像是栩栩如生地正在進行著喔！

candle
['kændl]

名 蠟燭

I saw Jack lighting the candles.
我看見傑克正點燃蠟燭。

captain
['kæptɪn]

名 陸軍上尉，艦長，領隊

Patty looked at the speaking captain.
派蒂看著領隊正在發言。

goose
[gus]

名 鵝，鵝肉

We are watching a goose flying away.
我們正在看著一隻鵝飛走。

monster
['mɑnstɚ]

名 怪獸，怪物

Pat felt the monster touching his shoulder.
派特感覺到那怪物碰他的肩膀。

complain
[kəm'plen]

動 抱怨，發牢騷

They listen to Jack complaining.
她們聽著傑克在抱怨。

5.其他動詞—Spend

2-42

Spend是花費時間或是金錢的意思，兩者用法略有不同：花費金錢是《人＋spend＋價錢＋on/for＋買的東西》或《spend＋價錢＋buying＋買的東西》；花費時間則是《spend＋價錢＋動名詞、地點》。

castle
['kæsḷ]

名 城堡
They spent a lot of money building the castle.
他們花了很多錢蓋這個城堡。

charge
[tʃɑrdʒ]

名 費用，價錢；動 索價
She spent two hundred dollars on handling charges.
她花了兩佰元付手續費用。

cure
[kjʊr]

名 治療；動 治療
I spent two hours curing the cat.
我花了兩小時在給那隻貓治病。

grape
[grep]

名 葡萄
We spent one week looking for the best grapes.
我們花了一星期尋找最上等的葡萄。

greet
[grit]

動 問候，打招呼
Helen spends ten minutes greeting every guest.
海倫花十分鐘跟每位客人問候。

6.其他動詞—take

2-42

Take只能表達花費時間，用法如下：《虛主詞it＋takes＋人＋時間＋動作》其中動作要用不定詞，也可以把動作搬到句首《動作＋takes＋人＋時間》，其中的動作可以是不定詞或動名詞。

hike
[haɪk]

名 健行；動 健行，遠足
It takes me ten minutes to hike up the mountain.
我爬上山需要十分鐘。

chief
[tʃif]

形 主要的；名 首領，長官
How long does it take to become the chief manager?
成為總經理要花多久的時間？

desert
['dɛzɚt]

名 沙漠，荒野
It takes us five days to get out of the desert.
我們需要花五天的時間離開沙漠。

develop
[dɪ'vɛləp]

動 發展，成長
To develop a relationship took him years.
發展一段關係花了他好幾年的時間。

granddaughter
['græn,dɔtɚ]

名 孫女，外孫女
Finding his granddaughter took him thiry minutes.
他找他的孫女花了三十分鐘。

7. 有助動詞功能的Have to

2-43

Have to是必須的意思，和助動詞must的意思相近，後面要接上原型動詞，《人＋have to＋必須完成的事》，就表達出一定要做到的決心和使命。

dawn
[dɔn]

名 黎明，曙光；動 破曉
I have to stay awake until dawn.
我必須保持清醒直到天亮。

gasoline
['gæsə,lɪn]

動 汽油
You have to find a gasoline station.
你一定要找個加油站。

guide
[gaɪd]

名 導遊，指南；動 帶領
We had to find a guide yesterday.
我們昨天就必須找個嚮導。

Germany
['dʒɝmənɪ]

名 德國
We had to leave Germany in three days.
我們必須在三天之內離開德國。

goal
[gol]

名 目標，目的
You have to set a goal.
你必須建立一個目標。

8.有助動詞功能的 Have to疑問句用法

想要得知必須完成的事情、或反問對方有沒有必要…時，可以用疑問句《Do/Does＋人＋have to＋動詞原型》，當人是《第三人稱‧單數》時，前面的助動詞用Does，其餘情況，用Do開頭。

chase
[tʃes]

動 追逐
Do they have to chase after me?
他們非得追著我跑嗎？

crab
[kræb]

名 螃蟹，蟹肉
Do we have to prepare crabs?
我們一定要準備螃蟹嗎？

gram
[græm]

名 扁豆，公克
Do we have to care about a difference of just one gram ?
我們有必要在意那絲毫的差別嗎？

German
['dʒɝmən]

形 德國的；名 德國人，德語
Does he have to learn German?
他有必要要學德文嗎？

9.有助動詞功能的Have to否定句用法

要說明「不用…」、「沒必要…」時，可以用have to的否定句《人＋don't＋have to＋動詞原型》，當人是《第三人稱‧單數》時，則要把don't改成doesn't。

hero
['hɪro]

名 英雄，勇者
I don't have to make myself a hero.
我沒必要把自己弄成個英雄。

herself
[hɚ'sɛlf]

代 她自己，她親自
She doesn't have to do it herself.
她不需要自己親手做這件事。

gun
[gʌn]

名 槍，砲
You didn't have to use a gun.
（那時）你沒必要用槍的。

imagine
[ɪˈmædʒɪn]

動 想像，猜想
I don't have to imagine; I know!
我沒必要想像，因為我知道。

hanger
[ˈhæŋɚ]

名 衣架，掛鉤
You don't have to use the hanger.
你沒必要用衣架。

10.接動名詞的動詞

2-44

一個句子裡不可以同時出現兩個動詞，所以，若有兩個動詞的狀況發生，要把後面的動詞改成動名詞或不定詞。有些動詞後面只能接動名詞，像是這裡的所舉的例子。

glue
[glu]

名 膠水，膠；動 黏合
He gave up using the glue.
他放棄使用那膠水了。

hole
[hol]

名 洞，洞穴
Joy avoids driving over the holes in the road.
喬伊避免開車駛過路上的坑洞。

gold
[gold]

名 黃金，金色
They kept looking for gold.
他們不停地尋找黃金。

guard
[gɑrd]

名 警衛，看守員；動 看守
The thieves avoid running into the guards.
小偷們避免遇見警衛們。

guest
[gɛst]

名 貴賓，客人
She enjoys having guests in her house.
她很喜歡家裡有客人。

11.接不定詞的動詞

一個句子裡不可以同時出現兩個動詞，所以，若有兩個動詞的狀況發生，要把後面的動詞改成動名詞或不定詞。有些動詞後面只能接不定詞，像是這裡的所舉的例子。

college
['kɑlɪdʒ']
名 大學，學院
I hope to see you in college.
我希望能在大學裡見到你。

government
['gʌvə·nmənt]
名 政府，內閣
She hopes to work for the government.
她希望能爲政府工作。

certain
['sɜtən]
形 確信的，某個
I promise to finish the work for certain.
我保證一定完成工作。

central
['sɛntrəl]
形 中心的，主要的
She tried to get to the central bank.
她嘗試著到中央銀行去。

hall
[hɔl]
名 會堂，大廳
I need to get to the concert hall.
我得到音樂廳那裡去。

12.可接動名詞或不定詞的動詞

同一個動詞接上不定詞或動名詞，可能會有不同意義。動名詞通常代表過去已經做過的，例如：《remember＋動作》表示記得做過…；不定詞通常代表未來將要進行，例如：《remember＋動作》表示記得要去做…。

heater
['hitə·]
名 暖氣機，加熱器
They remembered to turn off the heater.
他們記得要關掉暖氣。

hardly
['hɑrdlɪ]
副 幾乎不
They hardly remembered washing the dishes.
他們幾乎不記得洗過盤子了。

hey
[he]

嘆 嘿，喂
We like to say "hey!" when we meet people.
我們喜歡在跟人見面的時候說 "嘿！"。

golf
[gɑlf]

名 高爾夫球運動
We love playing golf.
我們喜歡打高爾夫球。

napkin
['næpkɪn]

名 餐巾，小毛巾
The waiter forgot to give us some napkins.
服務生忘了給我們一些餐巾了。

1.-ing

2-45

用現在分詞當形容詞，可以讓對方更能想像、體會你所形容的人事物。形容的對象通常是無生命的事或物，因為本身的條件而引起別人的情緒感覺，是「讓人覺得…的」。屬於外界的想法。

guy
[gaɪ]

名 傢伙，小子，人
Ben is a boring guy.
班是個無聊的傢伙。

confuse
[kən'fjuz]

動 使困惑，混淆
The story is confusing.
這故事很令人疑惑。

movement
['muvmənt]

名 運動，活動，動作
It was a surprising movement.
那是個驚人的動作。

report
[rɪ'port]

名 動 報導，報告
I read an interesting report.
我讀了一個有趣的報告。

repair
[rɪ'pɛr]

名 修補，修理；動 修理
Repairing cars is a tiring job.
修車是個累人的工作。

2-45

想讓對方能想像體會你所形容的人事物，也可以用過去分詞當形容詞，而形容的對象，因為外在的條件而造成自身的情緒感受，是「感到…」，屬於每個人自己內在的感受、體會。

chart
[tʃɑrt]

動 繪製圖表；名 圖，圖表
I am bored of making charts.
我對於製作圖表感到很無聊。

growth
[groθ]

名 成長，發育，發展
He is surprised to see his son's growth.
他看到他兒子的成長很驚喜。

humid
['hjumɪd]

形 潮濕的
Mandy is tired of the humid weather.
曼蒂對潮濕的天氣感到厭煩。

host
[host]

名 主人；動 主辦，主持
She is excited about hosting the party.
她對主辦派對感到興奮。

Hong Kong
[hoŋ koŋ]

名 香港
Laura is interested in visiting Hong Kong.
萊拉對於去香港很有興趣。

1.關係代名詞是主格 / 受格

2-46

把兩句併做一句，就可以俐落地表達所有想說的訊息，用《對象＋形容話題…》補充說明。若對象是人，用who當關係代名詞；對象是事或物，用which或that。關係代名詞是主格時，不可省略，但作受詞時，是可以省略的

chairman
['tʃɛrmən]

名 主席，議長
The chairman is Lucy's dad. He is nice.
→ The chairman who is nice is Lucy's dad.
那位主席是露西的父親。他很和善。
→ 那位和善的主席是露西的父親。

purse
[pɝs]

名 錢包，提包

She bought a purse. It was expensive.

→ The purse that she bought is expensive.

她買了個錢包。那錢包很貴。

→ 她買的錢包很貴。

childish
['tʃaɪldɪʃ]

形 孩子氣的，幼稚的

I have a classmate. She is very childish.

→ I have a classmate who is very childish.

我有個同學。她非常幼稚。

→ 我有個非常幼稚的同學。

hop
[hɑp]

動 跳過，躍過；名 麻藥

The rabbit is hopping around. It is David's.

→ The rabbit (that is) hopping around is David's.

那隻兔子跳來跳去的。牠是大衛的。

→ 那隻跳來跳去的兔子是大衛的。

insect
['ɪnsɛkt]

名 蟲，昆蟲

The insects were alive. We saw them.

→ The insects we saw were alive.

那些昆蟲是活的。我們看見了它們。

→ 我們看見的那些昆蟲是活的。

《對象＋形容話題…》形容話題是用關係代名詞引導的句子，當對象是另一句話裡面的所有格時，不論是人或物都要用whose（…的）當作關係代名詞。whose不可省略。

hunter
['hʌntɚ]

名 獵人

They saw the hunter. His hair was brown.

→ They saw the hunter whose hair was brown.

他們看見一個獵人。他的頭髮是棕色的。

→ 他們看見一位頭髮是棕色的獵人。

sea
[si]

名 海

I went to the sea. Its color was deep blue.

→ I went to the sea whose color was deep blue.

我去了海（邊）。海的顏色是深藍色。

→ 我去了一片深藍色的海（邊）。

height
[haɪt]

名 高度

Peter has a brother. His height is 180cm.

→ Peter has a brother whose height is 180cm.

彼得有個弟弟。他身高一百八十公分。

→ 彼得有個身高一百八十公分的弟弟。

fashionable
['fæʃənəbl̩]

形 時尚的，流行的

Phoebe showed me a hat. Its design was fashionable.

→ Phoebe showed me a hat whose design was fashionable.

菲比給我看了一頂帽子。帽子的設計很時尚。

→ 菲比給我看了一頂設計很時尚的帽子。

188

hammer
['hæmɚ]

名 鎯頭，鐵鎚

We brought a hammer. Its handle was yellow.

→ We brought a hammer whose handle was yellow.

我們帶了一支鐵鎚。鐵鎚的把柄是黃色的。

→ 我們帶了一支把柄是黃色的鐵鎚。

3.that的省略用法

2-46

在某些特定動詞後面所接的that子句，可以省去關係代名詞that，至於是哪些動詞，則只能多學多熟悉囉！

grandson
['grænd,sʌn]

名 孫子，外孫

She hopes (that) her grandson can come.

她希望她的孫子可以來。

ill
[ɪl]

形 生病的，不健康的

They realized (that) she feels ill.

她們發現她感覺病了。

hers
[hɝz]

代 她的某物

I think (that) the purse is hers.

我認為這錢包是她的。

God
[gɑd]

名 上帝，造物主

We feel (that) God is listening.

我們感覺到上帝在傾聽。

hunt
[hʌnt]

動 追捕，獵取；名 打獵

He said (that) he won't go hunting.

他說他部會去打獵。

4.what的用法

間接疑問就是《what＋對象＋動作》，配合上間接疑問前的動作《人＋動作＋間接疑問》，就可以用來說明某人做了什麼、說了什麼。

require
[rɪ'kwaɪr]

動 要求，需要
I don't have what you require.
我沒有你需要的(東西)。

favorite
['fevərɪt]

形 最喜愛的；名 中意的人（或物）
She doesn't know what his favorite dish is.
她不知道他的最喜歡的菜是什麼。

reply
[rɪ'plaɪ]

動 答覆；名 回答，答覆
They don't remember what he replied.
他們不記得他回覆了什麼。

musician
[mju'zɪʃən]

名 音樂家，音樂人
We catch what the musician is saying.
我們懂那位音樂家說的話。

brush
[brʌʃ]

動 刷；名 刷子
She shows me what she painted with the brush.
她給我看她用刷子畫了什麼。

5.why的用法

有時候用直接用問句詢問原因，會有一種質疑別人的感覺，想要避免這種咄咄逼人的口氣時，可以用間接問句《why＋對象＋動作》，這樣就可以溫柔、平和的問出想要的答案。

mark
[mɑrk]

動 標示
I know why he marked my name.
我知道為什麼他要標記我的名字。

stand
[stænd]

動 站立
They wonder why he is standing.
他們在想他為什麼站著。

mud
[mʌd]

名 泥土，泥漿
I want to know why she has so much mud on her shoes.
我想知道她鞋子上怎麼會這麼多泥土。

ball
[bɔl]

名 球
I forgot why I brought the ball.
我忘了為什麼我要帶著球來。

gym
[dʒɪm]

名 體育館，健身房
I understand why she's always at the gym.
我了解她為什麼總是在健身房了。

索引

chance	83	collect	51	date	125
change	16	college	184	daughter	32
channel	178	color	107	dawn	181
chapter	178	come	33	day	104
charge	180	comfortable	141	dead	102
chart	186	comic	27	deal	156
chase	182	common	141	dear	100
cheap	111	complain	179	December	83
cheat	126	computer	13	decide	95
check	30	confident	122	decision	150
cheer	142	Confucius	122	decorate	159
cheese	109	confuse	185	delay	150
chess	171	convenient	140	delicious	89
chicken	102	cook	32	dentist	159
chief	180	cookie	50	department store	58
child	39	cool	141	depend	149
childhood	171	copy	31	describe	150
childish	187	correct	31	desert	181
China	128	cost	102	design	157
Chinese	79	couch	32	desk	133
chocolate	8	count	136	dessert	169
choose	165	country	52	develop	181
chopsticks	46	cousin	15	diamond	168
Christmas	13	cover	143	diary	162
church	123	cow	134	dictionary	59
circle	99	crab	182	die	71
citizen	177	crayon	121	diet	163
city	24	crazy	44	different	135
clap	178	cross	136	difficult	113
class	49	crowd	165	dig	132
classmate	60	cry	14	dinner	13
classroom	50	culture	121	direction	160
clean	130	cup	55	dirty	68
clear	89	cure	180	discuss	162
climb	142	curious	164	dish	32
clock	50	customer	162	distance	163
close	73	cut	95	do (does,did,done)	45
clothes	55	cute	19	doctor (Dr.)	17
cloudy	104			dog	18
club	88	【D】		doll	21
coat	56			dollar	91
coffee	13	dance	15	dolphin	160
Coke	105	dangerous	103	door	41
cold	123	dark	69	down	135
		data	151		

machine	131	modern	17	nice	41
magazine	160	moment	77	niece	23
magic	81	Monday	31	night	31
mail	38	money	55	nine	72
mailman (mail carrier)		monkey	89	nineteen	147
	140	monster	179	ninety	138
main	172	month	37	no	144
make	63	monthly	71	nobody	108
mall	167	moon	76	nod	143
man	85	more	115	noise	44
many	135	morning	73	noodle	85
map	81	most	101	noon	132
March	107	mother (mom;mommy)		north	110
mark	190		44	nose	107
market	42	motorcycle	68	not	39
married	29	mountain	101	notebook	9
marry	31	mouse	52	nothing	108
math	114	mouth	111	notice	46
matter	138	move	36	novel	25
may (might)	67	movement	185	November	131
May	109	movie	57	now	37
maybe	52	Mr.	124	number	77
meal	96	Mrs.	72	nurse	26
mean	95	Ms.	65		
meat	139	mud	191	**【O】**	
medicine	127	museum	74		
medium	145	music	25	o'clock	148
meet	98	musician	190	October	127
meeting	38	must	94	of	66
melon	166			off	108
memory	152	**【N】**		office	11
menu	75			officer	87
microwave	40	name	58	often	63
midnight	172	napkin	185	oil	131
mile	139	national	57	OK	78
milk	49	natural	121	old	21
million	123	near	59	on	48
mind	84	necessary	172	once	128
mine	168	neck	75	one	87
minute	71	need	47	open	47
miss	128	nephew	57	or	148
Miss	77	never	106	orange	49
mistake	73	new	15	order	11
model	121	news	65	other	71
		next	39	out	60

road	31	seven	85	slippers	167
rob	166	seventeen	100	slow	115
robot	166	seventh	143	small	68
ROC	125	seventy	146	smart	24
roll	161	several	88	smell	64
roof	161	shake	165	smile	90
room	80	shall	116	smoke	27
rope	170	shape	144	snack	109
rose	30	share	45	snake	137
round	26	shark	155	snow	129
row	172	she (her,hers,herself)		snowy	153
rule	80		96	so	99
ruler	145	sheep	53	soccer	152
run	11	ship	93	socks	102
Russia	161	shirt	23	sofa	109
		shop	49	some	33

[S]

		shopkeeper	101	someone (somebody)	
		short	9		65
sad	32	should	106	something	64
safe	93	shoulder	143	sometimes	85
salad	55	shout	151	son	9
sale	91	show	68	song	19
salesman	168	shut	169	soon	79
salt	74	shy	112	sorry	41
same	57	sick	149	sound	77
sandwich	51	side	69	soup	91
Saturday	78	sidewalk	109	south	59
save	27	sign	167	space	111
say	128	silent	169	spaghetti	120
school	79	simple	60	speak	22
sea	188	since	126	speaker	18
season	105	sing	12	special	58
seat	56	singer	20	spell	70
second	57	sir	61	spend	147
secretary	158	sister	21	spoon	117
see	12	sit	47	sport	53
seldom	115	six	51	spring	50
selfish	159	sixteen	82	square	131
sell	147	sixth	95	stage	120
semester	163	sixty	104	stand	190
send	40	size	97	star	129
senior high school	17	skate	167	start	35
sentence	77	skirt	97	station	74
September	95	sleep	52	stay	14
serious	84				

memo

決勝英單

中學必背單字1500

中學三年單字、文法一次雙效搞定！

[25K+MP3]

英語大全 **05**

▼ 著　　者　**里昂**

▼ 發 行 人　**林德勝**

▼ 出版發行　**山田社文化事業有限公司**
　　　地址　臺北市大安區安和路一段112巷17號7樓
　　　電話　02-2755-7622
　　　傳真　02-2700-1887

▼ 郵政劃撥　**19867160號　大原文化事業有限公司**

▼ 總 經 銷　**聯合發行股份有限公司**
　　　地址　新北市新店區寶橋路235巷6弄6號2樓
　　　電話　02-2917-8022
　　　傳真　02-2915-6275

▼ 印　　刷　**上鎰數位科技印刷有限公司**

▼ 法律顧問　**林長振法律事務所　林長振律師**

▼ 書＋MP3　**定價　新台幣 320 元**

▼ 初　　版　**2019 年 6 月**

© ISBN : 978-986-246-547-9
2019, Shan Tian She Culture Co. , Ltd.